THE ART OF
WOODWORKING

AND FURNITURE APPRECIATION

THE ART OF
WOODWORKING

AND FURNITURE APPRECIATION

LASZLO KATZ

P.F.C. PUBLISHING CO., INC. in cooperation with P.F.C. WOODWORKING CO., INC., NEW YORK.

LIBRARY OF CONGRESS CATALOG CARD #77-107857
ISBN 0-9603830
SECOND REVISED EDITION 1980

FRENCH XVIII CENTURY

Magnificent Rosewood Secretaire with porcelain and ormolu embellishments, made by Martin Carlin.

The Metropolitan Museum of Art, Gift of the
Samuel H. Kress Foundation, 1958

BEHOLD, WHAT CRAFTSMENS HANDS HAVE WROUGHT.

Eighteenth and Nineteenth century
carpenter's and cabinetmaker's tools.
Author's Collection

INTRODUCTION

Because of the sheer enormity of the
subject, a work such as this cannot be
anything but a humble effort to establish a
memorial to the magnificent ages when skill and
craftsmanship were the most respected attributes.
Well made decorative and functional furniture
was treasured for generations, thus giving us
a heritage of museum pieces and antiques.
In contrast, our contemporary mass-produced
furniture is justifiably regarded as
disposable, and the only requirement to
prove skill lies in buying a membership
card in one or another organization.
The pride of accomplishment seems to come
from the size of the pay in the envelope.
However, I believe that this dinosaur of
trades is not extinct yet, and if you are the
personality who would prefer well made furniture,
designed to your taste and needs, rather
than factory made (and would rather hang
an original oil painting on your wall
instead of a cheap print), then today's trend
may yet be reversed, because "demand creates
supply," and this book is dedicated to you.
Cabinetmaking as a hobby is rewarding to everyone,
especially to those people whose everyday work
does not involve much physical endeavor.
To the youth of today I offer this trade as an
alternative to being a clerk in an office, or
operating a machine in a factory.
There should be a program, government
or private, whereby retired craftsmen would
be encouraged to teach in trade schools.
Never mind that he is not a college graduated
pedagogue, he has in his heart, his mind and
hands the skill and experience of generations.
It is immoral to let this treasure go to waste.
But you may be interested only in fine
furniture and antiques. I have tried to
assemble the greatest treasures of
cabinetmaking's history, as well as some of the
representative styles, followed by a not too
technical description of tools, woods, wood joints
and finishing used on some of these fine pieces.
With the hope that I have accomplished what you expect
from such a book as this — and I profess to nothing,
except to being a cabinetmaker —
I humbly offer this work for your kind consideration.

LASZLO KATZ

BIBLIOGRAPHY

THE BIBLE

ILLUSTRATED HISTORY OF FURNITURE
Frederick Litchfield

FURNITURE IN THE ANCIENT WORLD
Hollis S. Baker. Macmillan

ANCIENT & MODERN FURNITURE
John W. Small. Geo. H. Palley & Co.

FURNITURE
Esther Singleton. Duffield & Co.

HISTORIC STYLES IN FURNITURE
Virginia Robie. Houghton Mifflin Co.

FURNITURE OF THE GREEKS, ETRUSCANS AND ROMANS
G.M.A. Richter. Phaidon Press

FURNITURE OF CLASSICAL GREECE
T. H. Robsjohn-Gibbings and Carlton W. Pullin. Alfred A Knopf

CHINESE DOMESTIC FURNITURE
Gustav Ecke. Charles E. Tuttle Co.

FURNITURE PAST AND PRESENT
Louise Ade Boger. Doubleday & Co.

FRENCH ROYAL FURNITURE
Pierre Verlet. Clarkson N. Potter Inc.

LOUIS XVI FURNITURE
Ernest Dumanthier. Albert Morance, Paris

WINDSOR CASTLE
Sir Owen Morshead. Phaidon Press

THE CONNOISSEUR CORONATION BOOK 1953
L. G. G. Ramsey F. S. A. The Connoisseur

A SHORT HISTORY OF ENGLISH FURNITURE
H. M. S. O. London

ADAM & HEPPLEWHITE FURNITURE
Clifford Musgrave. Taplinger Publishing Co.

SHERATON FURNITURE
Ralph Fastnedge. Thomas Yoseloff

REGENCY FURNITURE
Margaret Jourdain — Ralph Fastnedge. Country Life Limited

GEORGIAN CABINETMAKERS
Ralph Edwards — Margaret Jourdain. Country Life Limited

A HISTORY OF AMERICAN FURNITURE
Marta K. Sironen. The Towse Publishing Co.

THE CABINETMAKERS OF AMERICA
Ethel Hall Byerkoe. Bonanza

OF ALL WHO LIVED

LOVED AND HATED

THEY LIVE FOREVER

WHO CREATED . . .

L. K.

In grateful appreciation to those who
with their skillful and craftsmanlike workmanship
created this beautiful and excellent book.

Edwin D. Orans of Mattwin Studios
for design and preparation for press

Judith Berkun for editing and proofreading

Lew Merrim for photo-technical assistance

Elwood Schnibbe for retouching

Grapho Typography, Inc. for typesetting (Helvetica)

Andrew Dirga of Murray Printing Company for printing

Herman Chidekel of H. Wolff Book Manufacturing Co. Inc.
for binding, and his overall counsel and guidance

Technical drawings by the Author.

LOVINGLY DEDICATED TO

PAUL, FAYE AND CLARA

CONTENTS

EGYPTIAN, PRE-DYNASTIC
Flint tools and implements: a flint saw
blade, many kinds of knives, cutters, scrapers.

Metropolitan Museum of Art   Rogers Fund 1916

QUARTZITE

GARNET

FLINT

NEOLITHIC and EGYPTIAN

Furniture has a great history. It has been
a part of mankind's environment for a very
long time. Its beginning was in the distant
past when the first caveman arranged twigs
lengthwise and crosswise and laid grass or
leaves over them, for the purpose of creating
comfort for himself and his family.
He even peeled off a large piece of tree bark
as a cradle for his child.
The mysterious human trait of gradual
development is interrupted at certain
intervals by great strides forward through
invention or discovery of new instruments.
Such must have been the splitting of flint
into tools. The flint gave man mastery over
the materials around him. Of these, wood was
most plentiful, easy to work with, long lasting
and readily adaptable to the human body and
its requirements for comfort. Eventually, man
tied a sharp stone to a stick, creating the
first tool that amplified his own power and
gave him the ability to cut and shape wood
more easily than with hand-held stones.
Flint made a very sharp and durable tool. A
long time after bronze tools were invented,
flint tools were still being used, even as
late as the 18th Dynasty in Egypt, about
3400 years ago. By then man had found that
he could shape one stone with another harder
one, and that a polished, sharp cutting edge
on a stone would make a tool as good
as the metal ones then available.

FLINT

OBSIDIAN

Tools, skills, and knowledge have come a long way since those early days, but with the rise and fall of civilizations, repeated throughout the history of mankind, the achievements of a civilization may be lost with its decline. However, the disintegration is seldom so complete as to destroy everything that was gained. Fortunately, no matter how unwilling the pupil, something remains with him and a new civilization rises from the rubble of the old. Today's crafts and knowledge had their slow rebirth during the Middle Ages. The science of archaeology in Egypt had not yet started. Medieval man had scant knowledge of great past civilizations or of the highly developed skills, including cabinetmaking, that made those civilizations possible. He would have known Homer's Odyssey, written about 900 B.C., where there is a beautiful description: "They put a chair for Penelope to sit by the fire. Wrought with ivory and silver, the craftsman Ikmalios made it long ago and fitted it with a footstool for the feet."

The most notable quote, I presume, is from the Bible, (about 14th Century B.C.) Exodus XXV/10, ". . . and they shall make an Ark of Shittim wood: two cubits and a half shall be the length thereof and a cubit and a half the breadth thereof and a cubit and a half the height thereof, and thou shalt overlay it with pure gold within and without."

We also see, in Exodus XXVI/15, ". . . and thou shalt make boards for the Tabernacle, of Shittim wood standing up, two tenons shall there be in one board, set in order one against the other." No doubt these specifications were given to a generation of highly skilled craftsmen.

We read (II Kings IV/10) when the Shunammite woman was preparing to receive Elisha, the Prophet, "Let us make a little chamber on the wall and let us set for him there a bed and a table and a stool and a candlestick." This was about 890 B.C. and shows that the average Hebrew home contained household furniture. Of course, if the common people had furniture of wood, the king must have had something better.

So the Bible says about King Solomon (II Chronicles 17 and 18), "Moreover the King made a great throne of ivory and overlaid it with pure gold. And there were six steps to the throne with a footstool of gold which were fastened to the throne, with stays (arms) on each side of the sitting place, and two lions standing by the stays." The throne was probably made by Hiram of Tyre, a great artist and King of Phoenicia. But why does the Bible say "The King made a great throne?" Did he design it, or did he have a hand in building it? It is possible, for many kings, prophets, and great men worked at trades throughout history. We are told that Jesus worked in a carpenter's shop until He was thirty years old. St. Mark quotes the people who heard Him preach, "Is not this the carpenter, the son of Mary . . . ." This was about the extent of the medieval carpenter's knowledge of the history of furniture and woodworking, but these crafts did not have their beginnings there. For that we have to go far back in time.

The prehistoric craftsman searched for a likely rock, of a shape that would make a comfortable tool when held in his hand. Much later he was to observe that when he chipped the same stone to a shape that could be tied securely to a stick, it became much more useful. Thus, the addition of the handle to the stone gave these early artisans greater control and leverage, and was a primary advance in the art of toolmaking. The stone/stick combination was the first compound tool of mankind, and its primitive developer used it solely for swinging or hammering. While he drove no nails with it, he did use this tool to pound posts into the ground, to mash fruits and grain, to hunt — to break open nuts and, in the beginning, no doubt to smash his thumb — just as his modern counterpart, the novice carpenter, is apt to do. As it became obvious that with a sharpened edge this type of tool would cut almost all the materials available to him, an era of new possibilities began, enabling the craftsman to cut and shape wood according to needs and desires of his community. He also continued to refine and improve the shape of the tool, increasing its comfort of handling as well as its efficiency.

The artisans who, over a long period of pre-history, brought about the development of handled tools, were primarily woodworkers, although among earlier civilizations the divisions between the craftsmanly trades were not so exactly defined. For the woodworker, making his own tools, (except for metal ones,) has always been part of his trade.

By the time the artisan could grind rough pieces of stone into finely shaped and functional tools he was no longer working haphazardly. Instead, guided by well thought out, advanced designs that took into account the weight, hardness, and grain of the stone, he was able to use all these elements to create beautiful as well as effective tools.

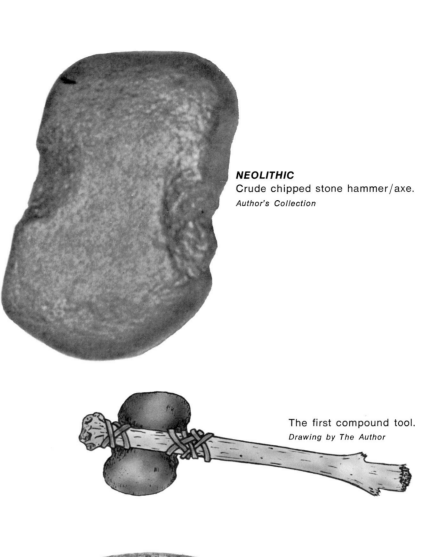

NEOLITHIC
Crude chipped stone hammer/axe.
Author's Collection

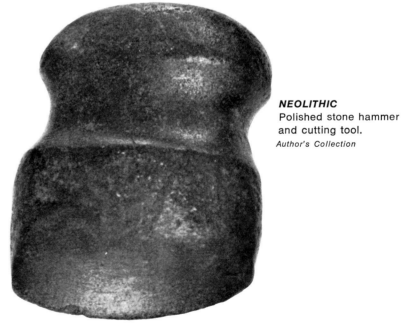

The first compound tool.
Drawing by The Author

NEOLITHIC
Polished stone hammer and cutting tool.
Author's Collection

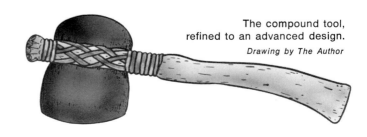

The compound tool, refined to an advanced design.
Drawing by The Author

PRE-COLUMBIAN

This beautifully shaped
stone implement may be
an early multi-purpose tool.
It has a comfortable "feel" to it,
so it could have been used
as a hand-held cutting tool,
but it also shows evidence
that it was struck with a mallet,
when used as a chisel,
and tied to a handle as an axe.

Author's Collection

EGYPTIAN, EMPIRE PERIOD, XVIII DYNASTY

Inscribed, probably mark of a Guild.
One of the high points in the development
of tools is this splendid bronze hammerhead,
notable for its exquisite shape and,
of course, its usefulness.
It combines the adze and the hammer,
and with only a flick of the wrist
the craftsman had at his command
a well balanced tool for cutting or hitting.

The Metropolitan Museum of Art
The Theodore M. Davis Collection
Bequest of Theodore M. Davis, 1915

PRE-COLUMBIAN

Bronze chisel.
Stone chisels had to be at least
a certain thickness and shape
so that they would not crack
under the blows of the mallet.
But when metals became available
it was feasible to make tools
thinner, lighter, and sharper.

Author's Collection

PRE-COLUMBIAN

Bronze cutting tool.
Exclusively a hand-held tool,
its possible uses were cutting,
chopping or carving, although it was
never used with a mallet.
The likeness of a lion is depicted on top.

Author's Collection

Egyptian drawing of daily life, showing cabinetmakers at work. The tools depicted are the saw, bow-drill, adze, rubbing stone, axe, and chisel and mallet. From a wall painting in the Tomb of Rekhmara, at Thebes.

Photograph courtesy of The Metropolitan Museum of Art

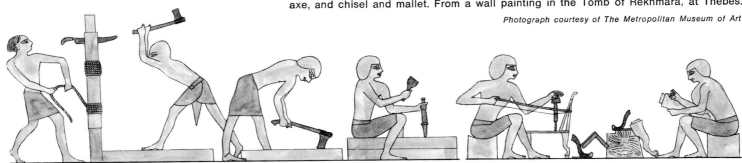

EGYPTIAN, 1503-1482 B.C.
An Egyptian saw with bronze blade engraved inscription. From Thebes, Valley of the Kings, Hatshepsut's Tomb

Metropolitan Museum of Art
The Theodore M. Davis Collection
Bequest of Theodore M. Davis, 1915

EGYPTIAN, UNKNOWN DATE
Indeterminate wooden object. It may have been a tool of some kind that we do not know today. From Lisht, North Pyramid.

The Metropolitan Museum of Art Museum Excavations 1920-1922 Rogers Fund, 1922

When the sun rose on the dawn of civilization in ancient Egypt, about the middle of the fourth millennium B.C., skills and crafts in the Nile Valley were by then far advanced. Copper tools were coming into use. By combining them with the flint tools of previous centuries, cabinetmakers were able to turn out magnificent furniture.

Tools and methods of working went almost unchanged for thousands of years. Most of their tools would be familiar today but we have found some implements that cannot be identified, and it is anyone's guess what they were.

Those fine and able craftsmen had to depend more on their own skill than on the workshop and tools available to them. Obviously, the screw was not known, and they had no vise, so wood to be cut had to be lashed with a rope to a post driven into the

EGYPTIAN, XVIII DYNASTY
Cabinetmakers using the adze and chisel to adorn a shrine with ivory and ebony ornaments. From a wall painting in the Tomb of Rekhmara, at Thebes.

Photograph courtesy of The Metropolitan Museum of Art

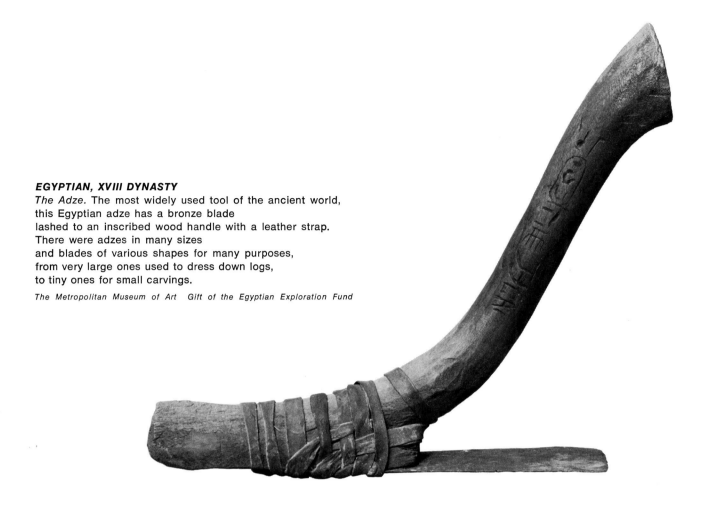

EGYPTIAN, XVIII DYNASTY

The Adze. The most widely used tool of the ancient world,
this Egyptian adze has a bronze blade
lashed to an inscribed wood handle with a leather strap.
There were adzes in many sizes
and blades of various shapes for many purposes,
from very large ones used to dress down logs,
to tiny ones for small carvings.

The Metropolitan Museum of Art   Gift of the Egyptian Exploration Fund

EGYPTIAN, XX DYNASTY

A sandstone rubber. These sandstone blocks
were used like sandpaper to smooth down wood.
Stones of various textures were used,
from coarse to very fine, the
last one used for polishing.
From Lisht, North Pyramid.

*Metropolitan Museum of Art
Museum Excavations, 1913-1914*

ground before it could be sawn. The copper
saw was an improvement over the flint saw,
even though it was of soft metal, and did not
stay sharp for very long. Probably the teeth
were recut with flint or some other hard
stone each time they were worn down.
Next in importance came the tool most
universally used in the ancient world, the
adze, an all-around tool used for planing,
shaping, carving, scraping, and so on, and
which, in some places, is still in use. I
have known old Roumanian woodworkers
who would come to town on market day, and
from freshly cut tree trunks scoop out a
kneading bowl or a washtub for the
children, which, of course, most of the time
served both purposes. We youngsters would
stand around for hours watching in awe the
precision and speed with which these
craftsmen used the adze to turn out their
wares. Although the simple adze is a most
efficient tool, I like to think, contrary
to accepted theory, that there must have
been some setup whereby it was attached to
a straight edge and then pushed or
pulled, as we use a plane today.
However, there is no evidence of that.
There probably was never a more efficient,
simple hand tool than the adze invented for
carving a leg or shaping anything. But even
today's well skilled cabinetmaker with a long
jointer or jack plane would be hard put to
duplicate the precisely straight and true
plank that served as a lid on
an outer sarcophagus. The prevailing theory
is that flat surfaces were dressed down
with the adze free hand, and then sanded
smooth with sandstone rubbers.

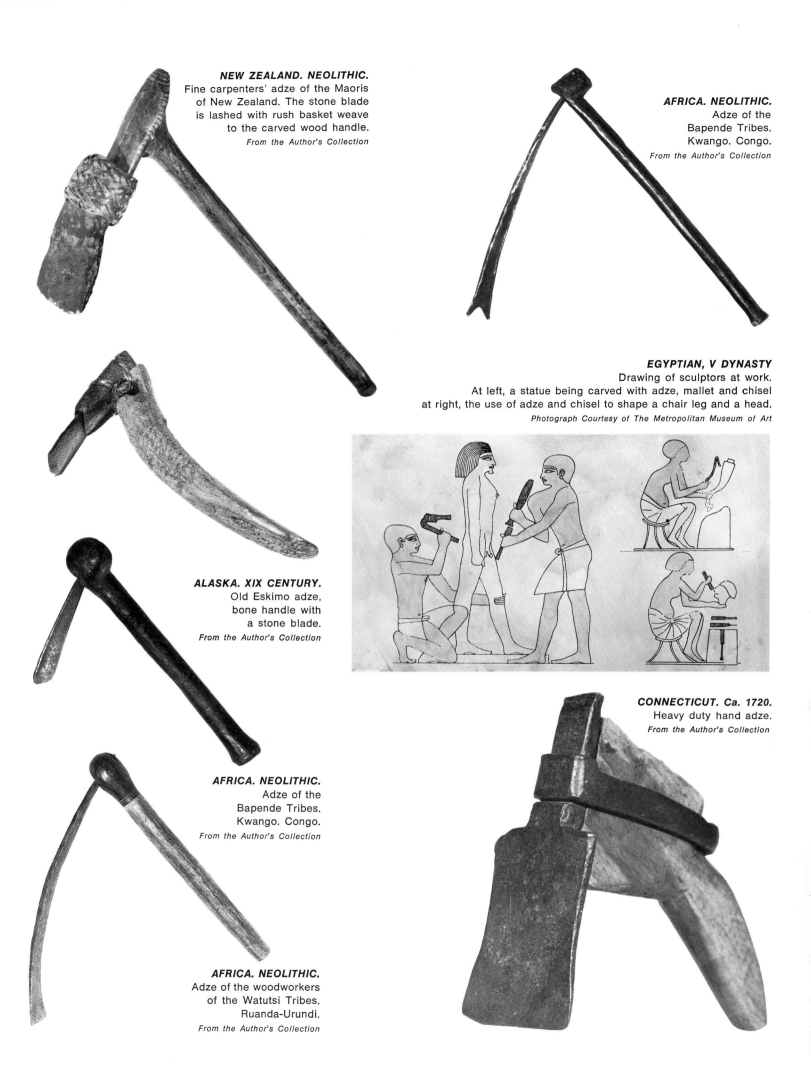

NEW ZEALAND. NEOLITHIC.
Fine carpenters' adze of the Maoris
of New Zealand. The stone blade
is lashed with rush basket weave
to the carved wood handle.
From the Author's Collection

AFRICA. NEOLITHIC.
Adze of the
Bapende Tribes.
Kwango. Congo.
From the Author's Collection

EGYPTIAN, V DYNASTY
Drawing of sculptors at work.
At left, a statue being carved with adze, mallet and chisel
at right, the use of adze and chisel to shape a chair leg and a head.
Photograph Courtesy of The Metropolitan Museum of Art

ALASKA. XIX CENTURY.
Old Eskimo adze,
bone handle with
a stone blade.
From the Author's Collection

CONNECTICUT. Ca. 1720.
Heavy duty hand adze.
From the Author's Collection

AFRICA. NEOLITHIC.
Adze of the
Bapende Tribes.
Kwango. Congo.
From the Author's Collection

AFRICA. NEOLITHIC.
Adze of the woodworkers
of the Watutsi Tribes.
Ruanda-Urundi.
From the Author's Collection

EGYPTIAN, XVIII DYNASTY
Wall painting from Thebes showing the method of drilling with a bow drill.
The seat of the chair is being bored for the rush webbing.
On the floor is an adze and a wooden square.
The Metropolitan Museum of Art

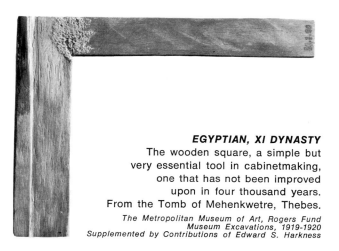

EGYPTIAN, XI DYNASTY
The wooden square, a simple but
very essential tool in cabinetmaking,
one that has not been improved
upon in four thousand years.
From the Tomb of Mehenkwetre, Thebes.
The Metropolitan Museum of Art, Rogers Fund
Museum Excavations, 1919-1920
Supplemented by Contributions of Edward S. Harkness

EGYPTIAN, CA. 1200-800 B.C.
The bow drill, a very efficient tool.
It has a granite cap and bronze bit; wood and leather are restored.
Below it is what probably was a measuring stick.
The Metropolitan Museum of Art Egyptian Expedition Rogers Fund, 1912

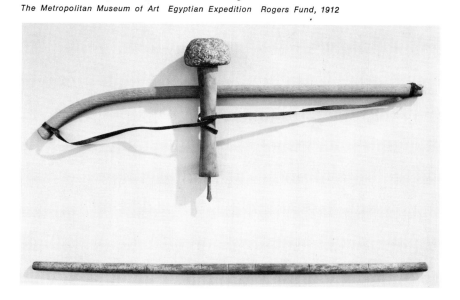

EGYPTIAN, XVIII DYNASTY
This chisel with a bronze blade was used for mortising.
The wide blade was needed as it was used with
a heavy mallet. Incised with the name
of Queen Hatshepsut (1503-1482 B.C.)
From Deir El Bahri, Thebes.
The Metropolitan Museum of Art, Rogers Fund
Egyptian Expedition, 1920-1922
Supplemented by Contributions of Edward S. Harkness

EGYPTIAN, LATE XI DYNASTY
Model of a chisel. This type of chisel with
a bronze blade was usually used without hitting,
or, on rare occasions, tapped with a light mallet.
The Metropolitan Museum of Art, Rogers Fund
Museum Excavations, 1919-1920
Supplemented by Contributions of Edward S. Harkness

The bow drill is an amazingly good tool,
very easy to make and very simple to use.
A very important basic tool is the square.
Would you believe this square is
4,000 years old? In fact, this tool
is so important in woodworking
that a cabinetmaker acquires the ability
to recognize by sight and touch if something
is square or not. The square is needed almost
continuously when working with wood.
Chisels (and chiselers) have not changed at
all for the last 5,000 years, in form and use
except, of course, for the metal.
The little change that has been made
occurred in the last hundred years.

EGYPTIAN, XI DYNASTY (CA. 2133-1991 B.C.) *(at left)*
Model of cabinetmaker's workshop. One man sawing, one man mortising, others working with adzes, sanding stones, etc.
From the Tomb of Meket-Re, Thebes.

Cairo Museum   Metropolitan Museum of Art   Egyptian Expedition, Rogers Fund

XIX CENTURY PRINT
A German cabinetmaker's shop where Biedermeier style furniture
is being made. The cabinetmaker in the center is mortising,
just as his ancient ancestor did some thirty eight centuries before him.
Author's Collection

EGYPTIAN, XII DYNASTY
Cabinetmaker's tool box.
Outside the box a chisel, a hatchet and an adze,
all with copper blades. On the box painted inscriptions
and probably a list of contents. From the Tomb of Ankh-Ef.

The Metropolitan Museum of Art   Gift of Edward S. Harkness

We have an idea what a carpenter's tool box contained, and what a carpenter's shop looked like, or at least what the ancient artist chronographer wanted to tell us. We are fortunate to have a wooden model of such a woodworking shop. It looks like a very comfortable community project, everybody sitting around and working nice and easy-like; one carpenter is sawing lumber tied to a post, others are using adzes, sanding stones for sandpapering or polishing. The most prominent person in the group is mortising with a wooden mallet and a chisel. He typifies the agelessness and universality of woodworking, which still continues in exactly the same manner in most parts of the world, even to this day. So they worked, turning out magnificent furniture that commands our admiration and respect for its shape and form, its refined construction and workmanship.

EGYPTIAN, CA. 3100 B.C.
Some of the earliest and finest examples of Egyptian
craftsmanship are these carved ivory bull's legs from Abydos.
These were supports for stools and beds.
To demonstrate the age of these legs better
we might mention that in Moses' time
they were almost two thousand years old.

The Metropolitan Museum of Art   Rogers Fund 1906

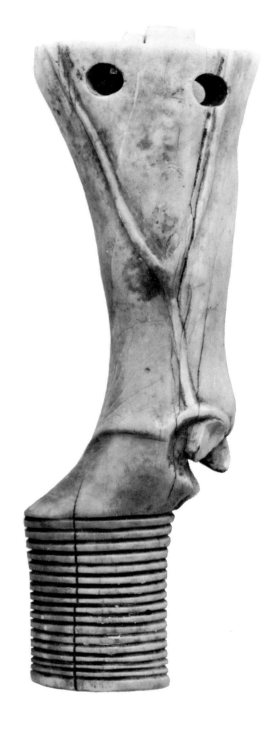

The legs from Abydos from about 3,100 B.C.
are fine examples of their highly
developed skill. These furniture legs carved
of ivory are in the shape of bull's feet.
They had a tenon on top, showing that
mortise and tenon, a form of joining
still used today, were already in use.
Some had holes bored into them,
and were lashed with leather straps to
the upper structure, or bed, as the case may
be. It has been suggested by experts that
this was done because glue was not yet
available. On the other hand, it has been
pointed out by others that one of the legs
was composed of two pieces of ivory joined
together, the reason for lashing legs
to the furniture was for easy disassembly.
Here again I would like to point out that
furniture made of wood came first, with
unshaped twigs for legs, then straight legs,
then shaped legs that finally evolved into
carved legs. However, after wood came
into common use, finer, rarer and more
expensive materials such as ivory, gold,

EGYPTIAN, CA. 3400 B.C.
This bed is one of the most ancient and complete pieces of furniture extant. Carved legs in the shape of bull's feet are tenoned into the mortised rails above. The rails are half-lap joined and are notched, probably for leather straps.

The Metropolitan Museum of Art
Gift of the Egyptian Research Account, 1912

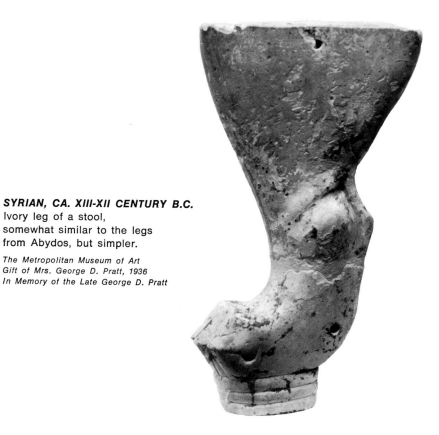

SYRIAN, CA. XIII-XII CENTURY B.C.
Ivory leg of a stool,
somewhat similar to the legs
from Abydos, but simpler.

The Metropolitan Museum of Art
Gift of Mrs. George D. Pratt, 1936
In Memory of the Late George D. Pratt

silver, and the like were sought and used. The ivory legs of Abydos give us quite a picture of design and workmanship. It is worthwhile to note the beaded cylinder on the bottom of the legs, because this feature continued to appear for the next 3,000 years on most furniture legs. Conservative designing, to say the least, but it does not distract from good proportions at all. It is one of the reasons why the chronological sequence is relatively unimportant when we delve into the ancient art of cabinetmaking.

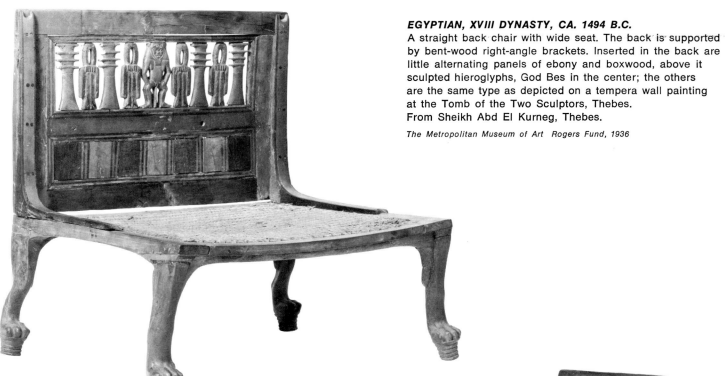

EGYPTIAN, XVIII DYNASTY, CA. 1494 B.C.
A straight back chair with wide seat. The back is supported
by bent-wood right-angle brackets. Inserted in the back are
little alternating panels of ebony and boxwood, above it
sculpted hieroglyphs, God Bes in the center; the others
are the same type as depicted on a tempera wall painting
at the Tomb of the Two Sculptors, Thebes.
From Sheikh Abd El Kurneg, Thebes.

The Metropolitan Museum of Art   Rogers Fund, 1936

These Egyptian chairs date from the 18th
Dynasty (c. 1567-1320 B.C.), but we can
safely assume that chairs looked more or
less the same fifteen hundred years prior
to this. As with the legs from Abydos, we
find the beaded cylinder motif on the bottom
of the legs. In shape, too, they are quite
similar, even though they represent lion's
paws instead of bull's hoofs. The legs are
mortised into the seat which is a complete
frame. For additional support there are
wooden angle brackets, which were bent by
either cooking or steaming until the wood
became soft and pliable. The softened
wood was then tied to a form which
held it until it had dried, retaining
the desired shape. They may also have tied
young branches on a living tree to
the form intended (much as we espalier
a decorative tree), and allowed them
to grow until strong enough for use.
The slanted back is also a frame and has
slats fitted into a groove to form a panel,
which is supported by vertical stretchers.
Here is a classic example of detail. We may
call it, as the old saw has it, "If you can't
hide it, feature it." As the back frame is
mortised and fastened with pins or dowels,
which could not be hidden from view, a

EGYPTIAN, XVIII DYNASTY
Chair and table.
Drah Abu'l Negga, Thebes.

EGYPTIAN, XVIII DYNASTY
"Senet" gameboard and men, Abydos.

EGYPTIAN, MIDDLE KINGDOM, CA. 2133 B.C.
Folding stool with leather seat.

EGYPTIAN, XVIII DYNASTY The little stool with food and drink on it. Drah Abu'l Negga, Thebes.

EGYPTIAN HOUSEHOLD FURNITURE

This simple Egyptian chair is obviously too low for the nicely proportioned Chinese-style Egyptian table. The folding stool is also a great piece of craftsmanship. Its bottom stretcher is flared out to meet the widened legs, giving stronger joints and the look of natural growth. The little stool is interesting in that the mortise is cut through, and because of its age.

The Metropolitan Museum of Art

EGYPTIAN, XVIII DYNASTY (CA. 1567-1320 B.C.)

This is the classical shape and form of the Egyptian chair, which appeared in many variations. Noteworthy here is the fine carving and workmanship of the lion's feet. The beaded cylinder detail on the bottom of the legs is retained. Here we can see how the pegs are capped with ivory discs as decoration. The larger disc in the center serves only to tie the others together in a design. The sloping back is supported by vertical slats.

Courtesy of the Brooklyn Museum

decorative feature was made of them by capping them with ivory, and sometimes with ebony. The panel has moulding around it, quite a feat considering that they had no moulding planes. This squat chair has cut-out hieroglyphs inserted into the back panel and framed by a moulding. In the center is the figure of the God Bes. The seats are reconstructed. The back of this chair is without any trim or decoration (a sort of Egyptian Provincial?). The table is amazingly Chinese in feeling, including the bead around all edges. On the table is a "Senet" gameboard which is glazed porcelain and inlaid. The folding stool looks so modern that it could have been made yesterday. It seems hard to imagine it is about four thousand years old, dating from the Middle Kingdom. There is also a little stool with a rush seat.

25

EGYPTIAN, UNIDENTIFIED DATE
Relief carving depicting
chair with gazelle-like legs
and table with turned pedestal.

Courtesy of the Brooklyn Museum

EGYPTIAN, XI DYNASTY (CA. 2065 B.C.)
Husband and wife sitting on a bench. This is an early example of the traditional lion's feet. The beaded cylinder is pyramid-shaped. The table, overloaded with food and drink, seems to have a turned pedestal base. Probably from Thebes.

Courtesy of the Brooklyn Museum

HITTITE, IX-VIII CENTURY B.C.
Showing woman and child.
A chair with curved back
and an undistinguishable table.
Carved in basalt.
From near Mar'ash.

*The Metropolitan Museum of Art
Purchase, 1891. Funds from Various Donors*

EGYPTIAN, UNIDENTIFIED DATE
These fragments of furniture,
probably a chair, are inlaid with ebony and ivory.
The legs have tenons on top, and the
sides are mortised for a stretcher.
The fragment of a rail is drilled for a
rope webbing. From Thebes.

*The Metropolitan Museum of Art
Museum Excavations. 1935-1936*

EGYPTIAN, XVIII DYNASTY

Drawing of daily life from a wall painting in a Theban Tomb, showing guests at a feast using the beautifully shaped chairs.

The Metropolitan Museum of Art

In this Egyptian "happening", ladies all bedecked are seen sitting on traditional Egyptian chairs being served by waitresses in very short mini-skirts. Here we have a stool of a very different design, which looks as if it has turned legs. There is no evidence that they had a lathe, but it is possible, considering the fact that they had the bow drill and the potter's wheel, from which the lathe is only a short step away. This bed is from the XI Dynasty (c. 2,000 B.C.). It is worthwhile to note the bull's legs are lashed to the frame, with rope in this case. The linen is from the same period. The headrest is of wood, and not the most comfortable kind of pillow. I tend to believe that this is a sign of an austere way of life, because pillows were known much earlier. Or maybe the ladies did not want their hairdos messed up? The beautiful toilet chest is an indication of how important cosmetics were to the ladies. The drawer is dovetailed, and it contains cream jars; in the top section is a bronze mirror.

EGYPTIAN, XVII-XVIII DYNASTY

A stool, one of the early examples of turned legs, with concave seat. From Drah Abu'l Negga, Thebes.

The Metropolitan Museum of Art   Gift of Lord Carnarvon, 1914

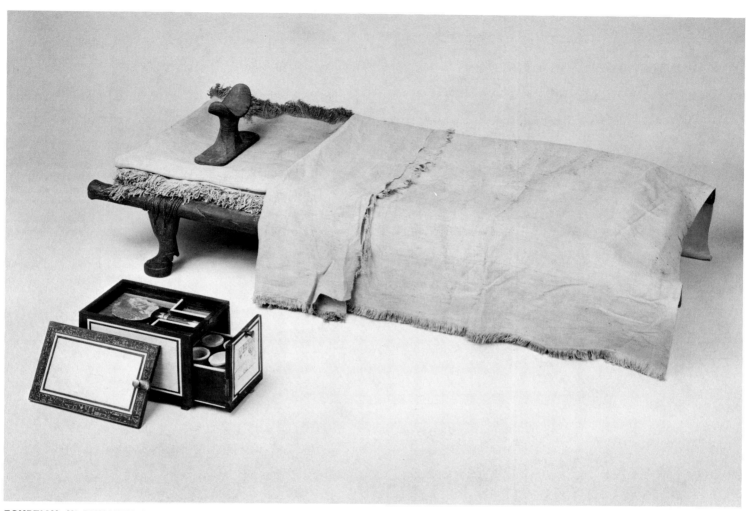

EGYPTIAN, XI DYNASTY (CA. 2133-1991 B.C.)
Bed standing on bull's feet that are mortised and
lashed with rope to the rails.
Headrest carved of wood. Middle Kingdom
Linen sheets, Deir El Bahri, Thebes. XI Dynasty
Toilet chest, Thebes. XII Dynasty,
during the reign of Amanemhet IV.

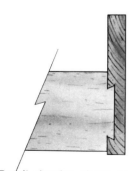

*Detail showing single dovetail
used on this drawer.*

EGYPTIAN, XII DYNASTY
The toilet chest is made of cedar wood,
inlaid with ebony and veneered with ivory.
The mountings are of silver.

EGYPTIAN, XXVI DYNASTY
Mother and child sitting on a stool with turned legs.
The table has the typical lattice work bracing.

Courtesy of the Brooklyn Museum

EGYPTIAN, 1361-1352 B.C.
From the Tomb of Tutankhamen,
an elaborately carved perfume container
on the top of a table carved in alabaster
but representing a wooden table with
splayed legs and lattice work bracing.
The Egyptians were aware
of the fact that the only geometrical figure
that does not ever change its shape is
a triangle, and they applied
that principle to brace furniture.
From the Valley of Kings, Thebes.

The Metropolitan Museum of Art
Photograph by Harry Burton

EGYPTIAN, XVIII DYNASTY
Dovetailed household linen chest. From the Tomb of Ra-Mose and Hatnufer.

The Metropolitan Museum of Art   Museum Excavations, 1935-1936

EGYPTIAN, XVIII DYNASTY
The lattice work bracing on this jewel box
is used as design; the wood is restored, inlaid with
glazed pottery panels. Belonged to the house mistress, Ren-Nufer.

*The Metropolitan Museum of Art
Museum Excavation 1934-1935   Rogers Fund, 1935*

EGYPTIAN, XVIII DYNASTY
A very fine chest of frame and panel construction
with bronze hinges for the lid and bronze shoes on the bottom of
the styles that extend down to form the legs. The carving is applied.
From the Tomb of Tutankhamen, Valley of the Kings, Thebes.

The Metropolitan Museum of Art   Photograph by Harry Burton

EGYPTIAN, UNDETERMINED DATE
Dovetailed wooden box.
This is still the proper way to dovetail:
there should always be half pins at the edge of
the work, seen at bottom of box, and the lid
must be cut through the center of a pin.
From Drah Abu'l Negga, Thebes.

*The Metropolitan Museum of Art
Rogers Fund, 1912*

The Egyptian household contained chests, and we may safely assume that storage chests have been very important with the ladies since the beginning of civilizations. Prior to that, during the primitive stone ages, it was the male who used to primp and decorate himself, but with the advent of civilization the ladies took over this role and have held it ever since. Soon women realized the need for storage and protection for their apparel and jewels, and thus evolved from the plain and crude, to the refined, inlaid and decorated chests and jewel boxes. Even our grandmothers and mothers placed great importance on their hope chests. This is not to say that men did not, or at least did not try to use chests. We can confirm our conclusions on how successfully, by examining today's wardrobes, bureaus and clothes closets.

31

EGYPTIAN, 1361-1352 B.C.
From the Tomb of Tutankhamen comes this chest veneered with superb parquetry inlay work,
the likes of which was not seen again until the 18th century A.D. when French cabinetmakers rediscovered the technique.
The frame is veneered with ivory and inlaid with ebony.

The Metropolitan Museum of Art Photograph by Harry Burton

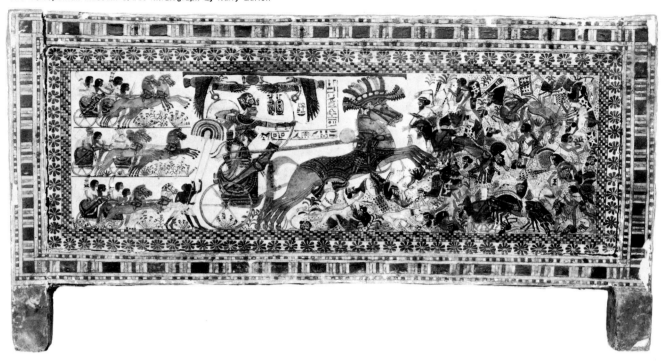

EGYPTIAN, XII DYNASTY
Detail of a box.
There is one board missing
and we have four types of
construction techniques revealed:
mortise and tenon, dowel,
mitered corner and shouldering.

The Metropolitan Museum of Art
Gift of J. Pierpont Morgan, 1912

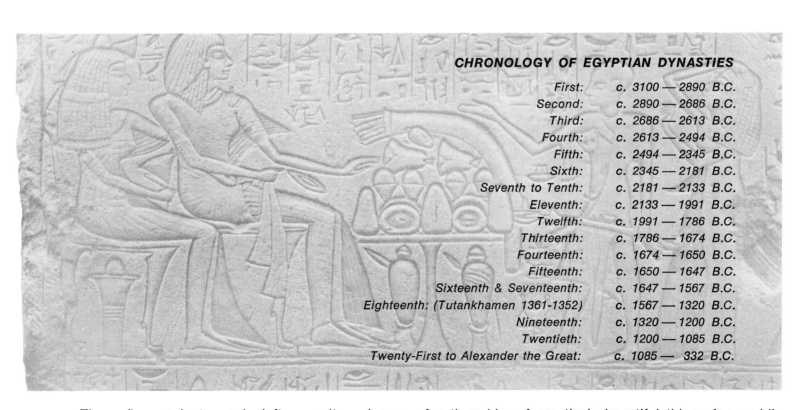

CHRONOLOGY OF EGYPTIAN DYNASTIES

First:	c. 3100 — 2890 B.C.
Second:	c. 2890 — 2686 B.C.
Third:	c. 2686 — 2613 B.C.
Fourth:	c. 2613 — 2494 B.C.
Fifth:	c. 2494 — 2345 B.C.
Sixth:	c. 2345 — 2181 B.C.
Seventh to Tenth:	c. 2181 — 2133 B.C.
Eleventh:	c. 2133 — 1991 B.C.
Twelfth:	c. 1991 — 1786 B.C.
Thirteenth:	c. 1786 — 1674 B.C.
Fourteenth:	c. 1674 — 1650 B.C.
Fifteenth:	c. 1650 — 1647 B.C.
Sixteenth & Seventeenth:	c. 1647 — 1567 B.C.
Eighteenth: (Tutankhamen 1361-1352)	c. 1567 — 1320 B.C.
Nineteenth:	c. 1320 — 1200 B.C.
Twentieth:	c. 1200 — 1085 B.C.
Twenty-First to Alexander the Great:	c. 1085 — 332 B.C.

Those fine ancient people left us quite a legacy of artisanship, of creatively beautiful things for worldly comfort, and what is most important, a legacy of creativity itself. Fortunately for us, they also believed in the hereafter, where one could enjoy the finer things of this world. That, combined with a favorable climate, gave us the opportunity to study the skill and handiwork of a great people of the past. Because our main interest has been limited to aspects of woodworking and furniture, we have merely scratched the surface of the Egyptians' contributions to the arts and crafts in the history of mankind. Further study will impart to the interested a world of knowledge and pleasure.

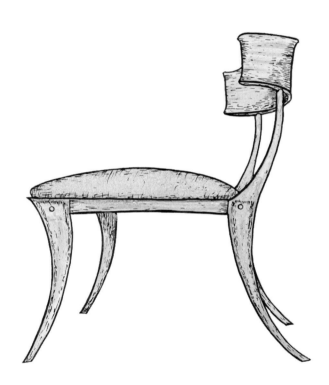

GREECE

The Greeks certainly had a word for it. They said "Klismos" and there appeared a chair,
majestically graceful, with sweeping curves and of pleasing proportions, ancient in years but as modern
as tomorrow's furniture. They also said "Dyphros" for stool, and a variety of stools appeared such that
today's designers of Swedish Modern or American Modern would be hard put to design anything more modern.
They said "Trapeza" for table, "Klini" for couch, and "Kibotos" for chest.

The magician's wands which created all these wonders were in the hands of countless thousands of
cabinetmakers, in the form of adzes, saws, bow drills, chisels, rubbing stones, and the like, backed by
centuries of learning how to work with these tools and wood. They brought the art of woodworking to a high
level of skill and quality, the standards of which are rarely achieved, and this only at great intervals
during the history of mankind. The numerous encyclopedias of ancient Greek life, the Grecian vases and
statuary, reveal to us a great wealth and variety of furniture. If you can, cast your eyes away from the
beautiful people represented on these vases and notice only the furniture of ancient Greece as it is used by
young heroes being entertained, if that is the word for it, by gorgeous maidens.

GREEK (ATHENIAN), CA. 450 B.C.
A lady sitting on a Grecian chair,
painted on a red-figured Lekythos (oil jug).

The Metropolitan Museum of Art
Fletcher Fund, 1926

GREEK, VIII CENTURY B.C.
Terra cotta figure
seated in an armchair.
This may have had
a footstool at one time.

The Metropolitan Museum of Art
Fletcher Fund, 1931

GREEK (CYCLADIC), CA. 2500 B.C.
This statuette carved in marble of a seated man playing the harp
shows one of the earliest predecessors of the graceful
Grecian chairs that appeared in the Fifth Century B.C.

The Metropolitan Museum of Art   Rogers Fund, 1947

But we are supposed to be interested
in the furniture only. If you are looking
for one detail in any work, you will
discover many more in the process,
for the appreciation of art and
artisanship grows on one and can
soon become an enjoyable habit and hobby.
The next opportunity you have
to examine Grecian vases and statuary
look for details, and remember: FURNITURE.

GREEK (ATHENIAN), CA. 480 B.C.
This red-figured Kylix (drinking cup) shows stools
with turned legs where a square block
was left on top of each leg to create a strong joint.

The Metropolitan Museum of Art
Purchased by Subscription, 1896

GREEK (ATTIC), CA. 430-420 B.C.
The Grecian chair in relief
carving on a marble vase.

The Metropolitan Museum of Art
Rogers Fund, 1947

GREEK (ATHENIAN), CA. 430-420 B.C.
A chair and a footstool appear on this red-figured Lekythos.
Attributed to the Eretria Painter.

The Metropolitan Museum of Art   Fletcher Fund, 1930

GREEK, CA. 470 B.C.
There are two stools with turned legs
showing on this red-figured Kylix.
Aren't they beautiful?

*The Metropolitan Museum of Art
Rogers Fund, 1923*

GREEK (ATHENIAN), CA. 480 B.C.
Detail of a red-figured Lekythos.
The legs on this stool
are constructed with a round block
on top for greater sturdiness.

*The Metropolitan Museum of Art
Fletcher Fund, 1924*

GREEK, IV CENTURY B.C.
This stool carved on a marble stele
has legs with rounded tops, and is very
similar to the one carved into the
frieze of the Parthenon by Phidias.

*The Metropolitan Museum of Art
Rogers Fund, 1911*

GREEK (ATHENIAN), CA. 430-420 B.C.
Lebes Gamikos depicting stools and chests.

The Metropolitan Museum of Art   Rogers Fund, 1907

GREEK (ATTIC), UNDATED
This red-figured Lebes Gamikos (wedding jug) shows a typical Greek chair and jewel chest.

The Metropolitan Museum of Art   Rogers Fund, 1906

The Metropolitan Museum of Art   Fletcher Fund, 1931

GREEK (ATHENIAN), V CENTURY B.C.
Eros offering the shirt off his back
to his lady love who is seated,
her hope chest at her feet.
On a red-figured Hydria (water jug).

*The Metropolitan Museum of Art
The Theodore M. Davis Collection
Bequest of Theodore M. Davis, 1915*

GREEK (ATHENIAN), CA. 430-420 B.C.
Detail of a Hydria
depicting a Grecian chair
and stool with turned legs.

*The Metropolitan Museum of Art
Rogers Fund, 1922*

40

GREEK (ATTIC), 550-540 B.C.
This folding stool
with inverted gazelle's legs
is seen in a detail
from a Panathenaic Amphora.

The Metropolitan Museum of Art
Rogers Fund, 1953

GREEK (ATHENIAN), CA. 430 B.C.
Ladies sitting on chairs,
and one holding a basket
and a small chest.
Is the guy with the wing
selling something?
On a red-figured Hydria.

The Metropolitan Museum of Art
Rogers Fund, 1917

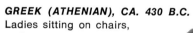

ETRURIA

Etruscan furniture was developed practically along with Greek furniture, and resembles it with only very slight variations.
There was a close relationship between Greece and Etruria from the earliest times which explains this likeness.
However, the important factor for us to remember is that furniture was made and widely used by the Etruscans who lived in Italy before the rise of the Roman Empire.

ROME

Roman furniture essentially does not parallel Grecian furniture, but rather is derived from it. The Romans changed it to suit their own taste, which was much more elaborate and ornamental. This couch (Lectus) and footstool (Scamnum Suppedarium), decorated with bone carvings and colored glass inlay, with heavy turned legs, are good examples of Roman style. The mosaic on the floor is from about one hundred years later.
But here we can see a person sitting on a stool with the same style legs.
The Romans carried the making of luxurious furniture to great extremes. Furniture was made of marble, gold, silver and bronze, and inlaid with precious stones and woods.
There was a table made for Cicero which cost one million sesterces to build. It was of Thine wood, which was held in highest esteem not only because of its beauty, but also for superstitious and religious reasons.
It was supposed to bring good luck, and it was sacred because the incense used by the priests was derived from this wood.

The unusual arrangement of the Roman dining room (Triclinium) contained three couches, each of which accommodated three reclining persons, with the table in the center, showing to what extent luxury and indulgence were manifested in some circles.

ETRUSCAN, ABOUT 600 B.C.
Model of a couch with pillows. It has a striking similarity to Grecian styles.

Courtesy of the Louvre

ROMAN, CA. 40-30 B.C.
Cubiculum (bedroom) from a villa near Boscoreale.
Roman couch and footstool date from the first century A.D. and are decorated with bone carvings and inlaid with mirror and colored glass.
The mosaic floor is Roman, second century A.D.

The Metropolitan Museum of Art

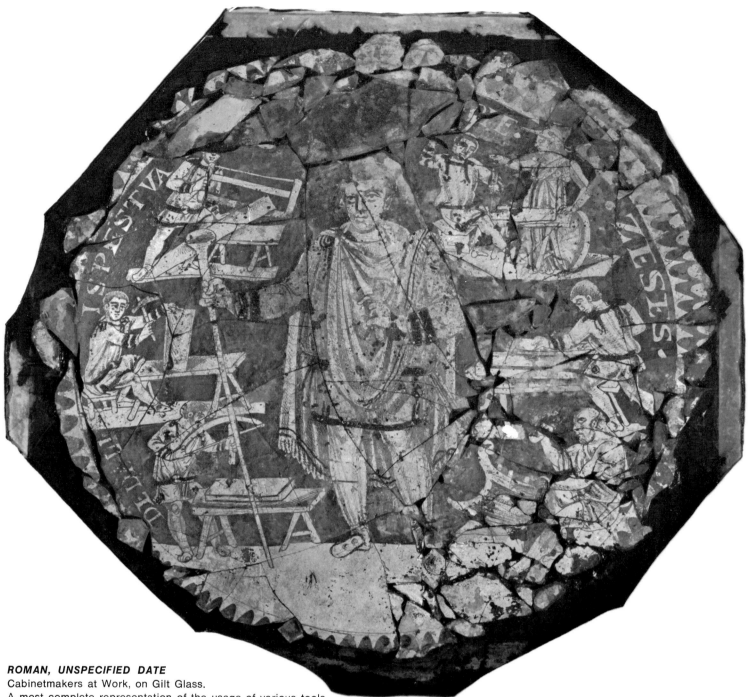

ROMAN, UNSPECIFIED DATE
Cabinetmakers at Work, on Gilt Glass.
A most complete representation of the usage of various tools
that have come down to us from Roman times.
Counterclockwise, from upper left:
craftsman using bow-saw (still used today);
man working with adze; another using a bow drill;
seated man working on a Grecian style chair;
cabinetmaker pushing a plane;
and, finally, mortising—
the man ready to strike the chisel
with a mallet while the lady is advising him.

Reproduced by Kind Permission of
The Vatican Library

Rome was the first large city,
and perhaps because of that fact,
the last empire of the ancient world,
where great masses of people suffered
poverty. However, that is the problem
for the social worker to solve.
With the fall of this decadent civilization,
the art of furniture making declined,
and the curtain fell on an important epoch
of mankind, the end of the ancient world.

Juvenile people descended upon the
civilized world looking for a place in the sun,
but instead brought down a
darkness that was to last for a thousand years.

CHINESE, CH'IEN LUNG PERIOD (1736-1795)
Screen panel, carved and painted in talc,
mounted on silk, rosewood frame.

The Metropolitan Museum of Art   Kennedy Fund, 1913

CHINESE. XVIII CENTURY. CH'ING DYNASTY.
Carved ivory figure of carpenter sawing a log. It is very interesting that the
saw he is using is so short, wide and obviously very heavy.
But it gave a straighter cut than saws used in the Middle East
and the Western world, which were longer, thinner, narrower and flexible.

Author's Collection

JAPANESE, 1757-1820
This print of a courtesan dreaming
shows a very elaborate Japanese table. By Shunman, Kubo.

*The Metropolitan Museum of Art
Bequest of Mrs. H. C. Havemeyer, 1929   The H. O. Havemeyer Collection*

CHINESE AND JAPANESE FURNITURE

Precious little is known of old Chinese and
Japanese furniture and furniture making.
There is evidence of a
commercial connection between
China, Greece, and the Roman Empire,
as far back as 200 B.C. Doubtless such
links benefitted all involved, but how much
influence they had on each other, one cannot
say from this distance. To recoin an old
phrase, no country is an island unto itself,
regardless of the time in history.

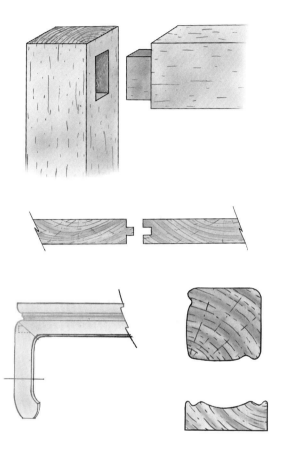

Cabinetmaker's chalk line (Sumitsobo). The chalk line was a basic tool of the ancient cabinetmaker. Middle-eastern, and later, western cabinetmakers wound their chalked cords around a stick. The inventive Japanese craftsman devised this interesting tool. The cord wraps around the wheel, and it goes through the chalk every time it is pulled out or rewound. In starting to build furniture they had to begin with a log and there still is nothing better to draw a straight line with on a crooked log.

Author's Collection

CHINESE, LATE MING DYNASTY (1368-1628)
Cabinet with inlay work cut into the solid wood.
The Metropolitan Museum of Art   Gift of Mrs. A. H. Wiggin, 1951

How far back Chinese cabinetmaking goes we do not know, but all signs indicate a very old and ancient craft. According to legend, the first cabinetmakers were Ly Pan and P'an Ku, who attained divinity. The millions of fine craftsmen who followed were second to none in skill and artisanship. Their pure and highly individualized designs and techniques were the result of many centuries of development. Almost all furniture was made of solid hardwood, and veneer was very seldom used. On palatial furniture where decoration and inlay were used extensively, the inlay was carved into the hardwood surfaces. Practically all frames, legs, rails, and edges have corner beads and often concave or convex molding carved into them; construction is almost exclusively mortise and tenon, and tongue and groove.

CHINESE, EARLY XIX CENTURY
Table with fine inlaywork of mother-of-pearl
incised into the solid wood.

The Metropolitan Museum of Art
Rogers Fund, 1909

CHINESE, CA. 1790
Dressing mirror, decorated with Chinese lacquer.

The Metropolitan Museum of Art
Rogers Fund, 1941

Chinese and Japanese cabinetmakers might
have used bronze tools which could have been
stamped made in Egypt, or Greece,
or vice-versa. Made in Japan?
There is also evidence that
there was furniture during the
Han Dynasty 206 B.C. — 221 A.D.
The K'ang was in wide use, a sort of
enlarged couch, or rather a boxlike platform,
for sleeping and reclining, not unlike the
Grecian or Roman couch. In the north, the
K'ang was built mostly of brick and in
winter it was heated from underneath on the
outside of the house. There was low
furniture used while reclining on the K'ang,
and regular size furniture used on the floor.
Finishing on the old Chinese furniture was
usually a very hard low luster wax, except on
decorative screens and some palatial
furniture, which were finished in lacquer.
The lacquer finished Chinese furniture became
the vogue in 17th century Europe because of
its great beauty, when the East India Company
started to import it. To reproduce it required
such high skill that it could not be
duplicated successfully for a long time.
It is believed many cabinetmakers made

furniture and sent it to China to be lacquered. Lacquer finish was also called Japanning, due to a minimal knowledge of the geography of the Orient. Many famous French, English, and Dutch cabinetmakers of the 18th century used lacquered panel inserts in furniture to great advantage. This superb lacquer finish was achieved by a long process: at first a silk gauze was glued to the finely sanded wood, then covered with a heavy paint made of buffalo's gall and powdered red sandstone. This was the base for red lacquer. For black lacquer, gray sandstone or powdered white clay (Kaolin), was used, colored black with soot. Vegetable dyes were used in the case of blue and the very rare yellow lacquer. When this paint was thoroughly dry, it was rubbed down with a wet soft clay sanding block until very smooth. Following that, the lacquer, consisting of a very fine gum resin derived from the sap of the Lac tree that grows only in China, Japan, Korea, and Malaya, was applied, and when dried it was again rubbed down with wet clay sanding blocks. This process was usually repeated three or four times. Finer furniture had six coatings, called "Lon-Tinsg"; but even eighteen coatings were not unusual. Next came the process of applying the beautiful Chinese illustrations; again heavy paint of different colors outlining the design was applied. Often gold or silver were added with a combination of colors, layer upon layer until the desired thickness was achieved. Then it was incised, as in the case of coromandel lacquer, rubbed down with horse hair pads, and polished with wax. Ivory, shells, marble and jade were also used extensively as decoration.

Words are hardly adequate to describe a process requiring such great skill as the finishing of Chinese furniture in lacquer, especially when we see a charming landscape on black lacquer, a Chinese pagoda-type house, a grotesque tree, a lake with a tiny boat on it on a moonlit night — surely a sight to behold, an achievement of artisanship!

GOTHIC FURNITURE

The furniture of the Middle Ages, whatever there was of it, was almost exclusively Gothic in design. The name Goth is quite a misnomer. Originally it was meant to be abusive. The Germanic tribes named Goths invaded most of Europe between the second and eighth centuries, leaving behind little in the way of reverence. Their name became a term associated with barbarians, uncouth and uncivilized people. In fifteenth century Italy during the Renaissance, they applied the name to this earlier style to denote that it was old-fashioned and uncivilized, but, in the last analysis, the style lent dignity to the name. The Gothic style originated in France about the twelfth century and spread throughout Europe. It is quite certain that the architects who designed the great cathedrals of that period also designed the furniture. Most, if not all,

Gothic furniture was made for church, monastic, or royal use. Domestic furniture was scarce, and what existed was simple and primitive. Most churches were built in the Gothic style even until very recently. This style is represented by pointed arches in contrast to the round Roman arches, rose windows decorated with trefoil and quatrefoil in many variations. Grotesque animals and foliage were also favorite decorations. The most important feature of the style, as far as furniture or wall paneling is concerned, is the Linenfold, which originally was supposed to represent parchment scrolls. As this was church furniture, belonging mainly to pious people, the scrolls represented the Bible before books were invented. The Linenfold concept came from the fact that there were linen hangings on the walls, tapestry in palaces, to reduce some of the chill in drafty old houses. Later when wall paneling replaced linen, they carved the Linenfold into the paneling and furniture. I still like the scroll explanation better. Furniture of this period, from approximately the twelfth to the sixteenth centuries, was made of oak and usually painted in primary colors. No doubt it did not look as dignified originally as it appears to us today seeing it, of course, with today's eyes.

FRENCH OR FLEMISH, XV CENTURY
Chest made of oak, frame and panel construction.
The panels are carved into a Linenfold design.
This is one of the earliest examples of paneling where
there is molding around the panels only on three sides: the two vertical and one horizontal, the top.

The Metropolitan Museum of Art   Gift of Mrs. George W. Cane, 1952

ENGLISH, LATE XIV CENTURY
Chest made of heavy oak planks and held together with pegs.
It has Gothic tracery carved into it.

The Metropolitan Museum of Art   Gift of Sir Joseph Duveen, 1921

FRENCH, EARLY XV CENTURY
Oak armoire with Linenfold paneling.
This cabinet shows a remarkable sharpness in carving detail.
We must assume that the craftsmen had well developed push-pull scraping tools,
although there are none now surviving for study.

The Metropolitan Museum of Art The Cloisters Collection Gift of Mrs. Cheever Porter, 1940, in memory of her father, John D. Cheever

FRENCH, LATE XV CENTURY
Armoire made of oak with Linenfold paneling.
Here, also, the molding on three sides of the paneling is very evident.
The beautifully carved astragal (the molding covering the joint between the two doors,
mounted on the door with the lock) is unusual on these cabinets.

The Metropolitan Museum of Art   Gift of J. Pierpont Morgan, 1916

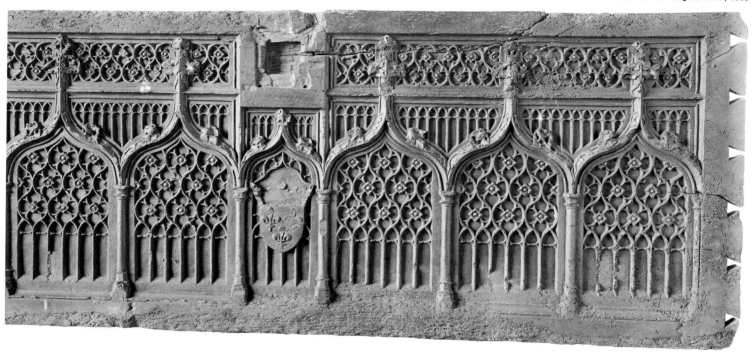

ENGLISH, 1300 A.D.
King Edward I's Coronation Chair. One of the most important and revered relics
of the Middle Ages, with the Coronation Stone, or Jacob's Pillow, under the seat.
This chair has been used for every coronation except one since that time.

Reproduced by Kind Permission of the Dean and Chapter of Westminster

One of the most important examples of
furniture of the Middle Ages is the
Coronation Chair, made for King Edward I,
1296-1300. It is a fine representation of the
style of the period, and holds the famous
Coronation Stone, (also known as the
Stone of Scone) which, according to ancient
legend, is the same one that the Patriarch
Jacob used for his pillow when Isaac sent
him away to find himself a wife.
"And he lighted upon a certain place, and
tarried there all night because the sun was
set, and he took of the stones of that place
and put them for his pillow. And Jacob rose
early in the morning, and took the stone that
he had put for his pillow and set it up for
a pillar, and poured oil upon the top of it,
and said, and this stone which I have set
for a pillar shall be God's House!"
(Genesis XXVIII/11/18/22)
The carved lions, supporting the chair,
are not original but were added later.
This is an awe-inspiring and venerable relic.

FRENCH, EARLY XVIII CENTURY
Engravings of various woodworking tools used in carpentry.

Diderot-d'Alembert. Encyclopedie Published between 1751-1772 Author's Collection

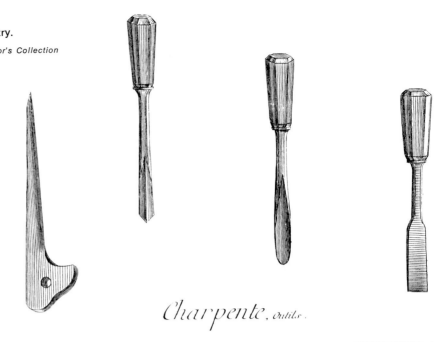

Charpente, Outils.

THE ARTIST
AND THE ARTISAN

In times of calm and prosperity the trend is toward progress and improvement. But in times of poverty and calamity the reverse is true. A regression sets in, people will do less for themselves, reverting back to the primitive. Skills will be forgotten until complete lethargy sets in, and hence, the Middle Ages, but when man did not have to struggle for his elementary needs, he strove instead for luxuries and surrounded himself with comfort and beauty. He demanded increasingly higher quality from the craftsman and artisan whose creations promoted a gentler way of living. He supported the arts and the artist, but he could not place any demands on them. The artisan and craftsman work by specifications, and have to apply all their skill and knowledge to create things representing in true life what the customer desires.
The artist only creates when he is inspired, and what his own inspiration and needs require. He is fortunate in that he can rely on his talent. He has few tools and needs little instruction. Michaelangelo needed a few brushes and buckets of paint to create the ceiling of the Sistine Chapel.
A mallet, a few chisels, some rasps, a large piece of marble and presto Pieta. The artisan, on the other hand, at the beginning of the Renaissance, had to recreate and improve on dozens of tools, furniture construction, relearn the nature of woods and how to work with them during a long apprenticeship, anywhere from seven to fourteen years. Apprenticeship was not the most humane institution ever, even in my time when it was only three to four years, but it did produce fine craftsmen and furthered the trade.

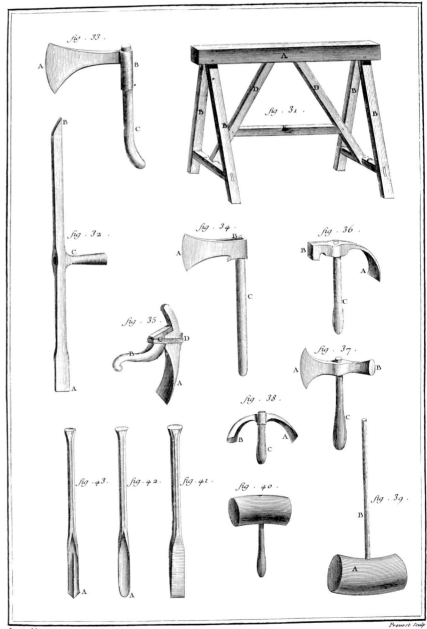

ITALIAN, XVI CENTURY
Woodwork on a Synagogue Ark, the cabinet
that holds the Torahs (Bible Scrolls).
Heavily carved with Jewish motifs
in the Renaissance style.
Courtesy of the Jewish Museum, London

THE RENAISSANCE

With the advent of the Renaissance
in Italy, the artist and the artisan
started creating with new vim and vigor.
This creative mood in Italy soon spread all
over Europe. Furniture was still designed by
the same people who designed the buildings,
and for the most part it resembled the house
for which it was intended. Grecian columns
and Roman arches were also in great demand.
Furniture was ''gessoed'' (a very thick paint
that dries hard as plaster, and can be carved),
painted and gilded. The Renaissance once
again raised cabinetmaking to the status of a
fine art, a situation that was to last for
the next four hundred-or-so years.
The concept that the wood of which the
furniture was made should be a decorative
feature, again gained the popularity it had
not enjoyed since ancient times.
By using many different kinds of woods as
decoration ''Intarsia'' or, as we better know
it, inlay work developed. ''Certosino work''
is a name supposedly derived from Carthusian,
a monastery where monks made beautiful
furniture, inlaid with very small mosaics
of ivory, cut to geometrical shapes,
and creating geometrical designs.
No doubt, Oriental and Byzantine influence
was responsible for these designs.
Carving was carried to great extremes,
not small and busy-like as it was to
become in the Baroque and Rococo,
but mostly large and sweeping flowers,
fauna, foliage, animal masks,
female busts, shells, and many more.
The great trend toward creativity
proved to be contagious.
Italian craftsmen were much sought after all
over the civilized world, such was the
admiration for the work of the Renaissance.

SWISS, XVII CENTURY
Architectural woodwork in a room from Flims, Switzerland.
Walnut, maple, sycamore, and other native woods are used.

The Metropolitan Museum of Art Rogers Fund, 1906

ITALIAN, CA. 1500
Folding chair from Lombardy,
showing Certosina work of high quality.
The chair is walnut inlaid with ivory and silver.
Furniture in the early sixteenth century
was built, we may safely assume,
exclusively for the church, royalty
or the very rich. Judging by the
amount and quality of workmanship
put into this chair with it's inlaid
Star of David, it was probably
made for the rabbi of a synagogue.

The Metropolitan Museum of Art
Gift of William H. Riggs, 1913

As the exchange of ideas, styles, and skills
continued, cabinetmaking flourished over most of
Europe. New methods were eagerly accepted and
improved upon. Styles were changed to suit a
growing variety of tastes. Great results
were achieved in Germany, Spain, France,
England, and in the Scandinavian countries.
In Holland and Flanders, where cabinetmakers
were fortunate to have the first choice and
use of exotic woods, such as veneers imported
by the Dutch East India Company, Dutch and
Flemish craftsmen were the first to use ebony
wood in Europe since ancient times.

VENETIAN, CA. 1780
Bedroom from the Palazzo Sagredo, Venice. The bed is carved and gilded wood. Ceiling attributed to Gasparo Diziani.

The Metropolitan Museum of Art   Rogers Fund, 1906

ITALIAN, CA. 1709
Cabinet on stand, veneered and inlaid with satinwood, rosewood and various other woods.
In the front are inserted eleven intarsia landscape panels made from different colored marbles.
Signed and dated by Baccio Capelli, Fecit Anno 1709 Fiorenza. Formerly at Kimbolton Castle, Huntingdonshire.
Enlarged views at right and below show veneer and marble inlaywork.
Courtesy Victoria and Albert Museum

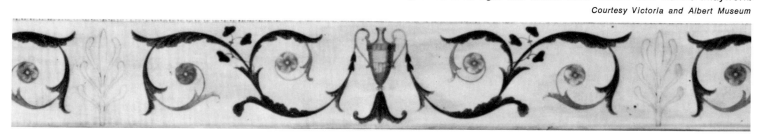

ITALIAN, XV CENTURY
Woodwork in the Ducal Palace, Gubbio. Walnut paneling inlaid with oak, beech, rosewood, and fruitwoods.
Designed by Francesco di Giorgio of Siena (1439-1502). Made by the cabinetmaker Baccio Pontelli of Florence (ca. 1450-1492).
It is a masterpiece of three dimensional design.

AMERICAN, LATE XVII CENTURY
Heavily molded and paneled
in geometrical designs,
with split turnery applied.
In Dutch style of the same period.
A massive and rugged, but still
a well balanced design, made of pine.
Probably from Massachusetts.

GERMAN, PROBABLY XVI CENTURY
A beautiful representation of Renaissance
carving on this cabinet from Augsburg.

FRANCE

The unique qualities and popularity of ebony
made many french cabinetmakers travel
to Flanders to learn the art of working and
veneering with this very hard and fine wood.
Its rarity required that it be used
as veneer rather than as solid wood.
Hence originated the name "Ebeniste"
which was given to French cabinetmakers.
The name stayed when they went back
to France with the knowledge of working with
ebony veneer. Eventually, all cabinetmakers
in France who worked on veneered
furniture were called "Ebeniste."
The Dutch cabinetmakers used, to a great
extent, beveled panels in frames, especially
on tall cabinets called "Kas."
Split-elongated or square prisms, half
turnings (turned posts cut in half
lengthwise) were applied to flat surfaces,
moldings were applied in many variations
of geometric designs. These designs had a
strong influence on the English cabinetmakers
of the Jacobean period, as well as on
the early American cabinetmakers.

FRENCH, EARLY XVIII CENTURY
Engravings of carpenters building; various woodworking tools.

Diderot-d'Alembert. Encyclopedie Published between 1751-1772 Author's Collection

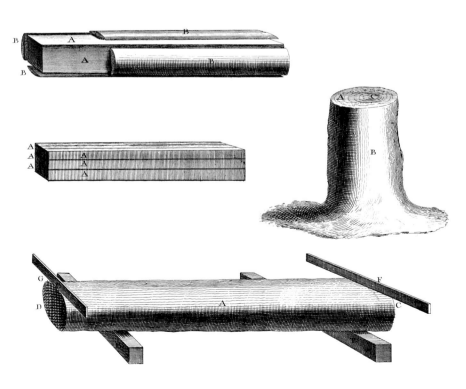

The styles of Louis XIII and previous monarchs were getting heavier, and it was time for a change. Then came the Sun King, Louis XIV, an ambitious monarch in many ways. He appointed a great painter and artist of the time, Charles LeBrun, as the Chief of Arts and Crafts. LeBrun created a great furniture factory at Gobelins, with several hundred of the best cabinetmakers, most of whom were foreigners at first, but were gradually replaced with French cabinetmakers. The craftsmen at Gobelins were exempt from the rules of the Guilds because they worked for the King and his court.

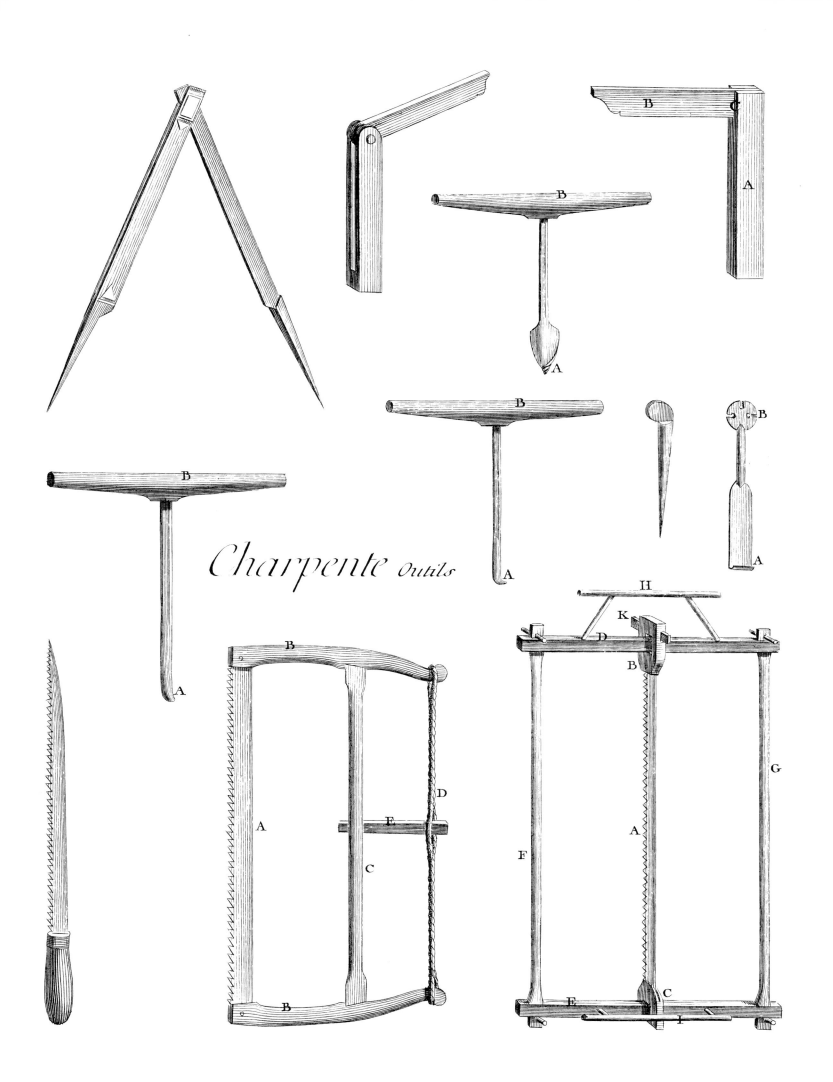

Charpente Outils

FRENCH, EARLY XVIII CENTURY
Engravings of a cabinetmaker shop; various woodworking tools, benches and clamps.

Diderot-d'Alembert. Encyclopedie Published between 1751-1772 Author's Collection

At this factory certain types of work were divided into separate trades. The Ebeniste made veneered and inlaid furniture and the Menuisier worked in solid woods, such as chairs and other furniture that was not veneered, but carved and painted or gilded. Eventually carving also became a separate trade.

Each piece of furniture was made by one master craftsman, one or two cabinetmaker helpers, and one or more apprentices, so actually there were many more people working at this factory, setting the pace with their fine workmanship, creating furniture that was to become the epitome of the art of cabinetmaking for ages to come. In competition with, and stimulated by the activity at Gobelin, French cabinetmakers achieved the zenith of furniture making skills. Rigorous apprenticeships were enforced on them. To qualify as a cabinetmaker, a sample work, usually a veneered and inlaid jewel box or small table, had to be submitted to a committee of older craftsmen appointed by the Guilds. If it was less than a piece of art, the applicant was severely criticized. If they found fault in workmanship, he could be ordered back to apprenticeship for a set period of time, after which he would have to submit a piece of his work again. The Guilds maintained these strict standards in issuing a license (maitrise) to practice as a cabinetmaker. Those who could not pass the test had to work as cabinetmakers' helpers all their lives. But they were not too proud to learn either.

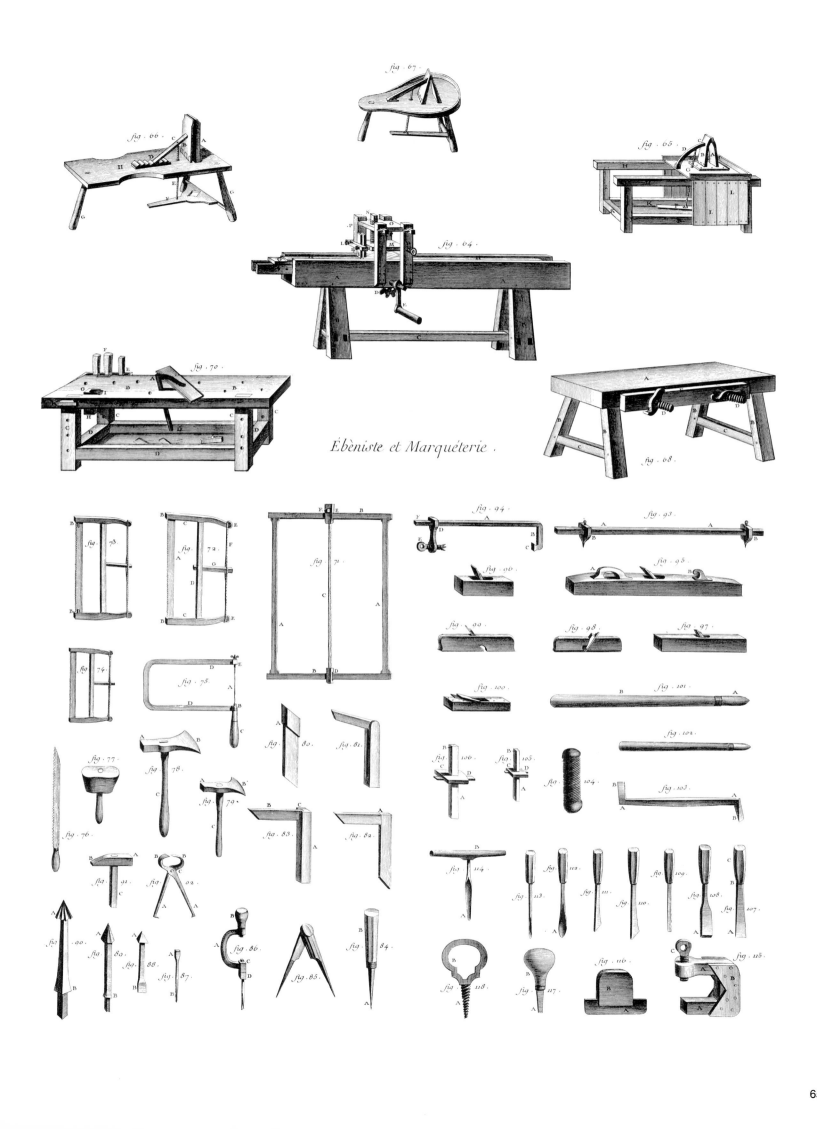

Ébèniste et Marquéterie.

Cabinetmakers, as mentioned before, were sent anywhere it was thought they could learn new methods of working, so-called trade secrets. They in turn would invite Italian, Dutch, English, and other cabinetmakers to France to work. After all had been learned from them, the foreign craftsmen would be sent back with rich rewards, and many times during the reign of Louis XIV, if the contribution merited it, they returned home with lifetime pensions. Of course, these methods did not escape the attention of other countries, especially the Barons and Electors (Kurfursten) in Germany. These nobles invited French cabinetmakers to work at their courts and teach the German cabinetmakers, who learned well. As a matter of fact, they learned so well that during the seventeenth and eighteenth centuries, at the height of the French cabinetmaking skills, German and Dutch cabinetmakers, including Oeben, Riesener, Weissweiler, Roentgen, and many others, were the greatest rivals of the famous French cabinetmakers of the time. Most of the styles of French furniture are known by the reigning monarch, who quite often influenced the style of furniture. The best known ones are the famous three, Louis XIV, Louis XV, and Louis XVI. Of course, this does not mean to say that, for example, when Louis XV ascended to the throne, all furniture making stopped, all old sample jigs and templates were discarded, and completely new designs began to be made. Probably many people would have preferred it that way.

FRENCH, XVI CENTURY
Elaborately carved armoire, made of walnut.
Courtesy of the Brooklyn Museum

FRENCH, XVIII CENTURY
Paneling with polychrome painted decorations. From a sitting room in the Hôtel de Crillon, 10 Place de la Concorde, Paris.

The most notable cabinetmaker of the period, actually one of the most famous, is Andre Charles Boulle, popularly known as Buhl. He developed and advanced the method of veneering with tortoise shell and brass to a high degree of perfection and skill. Boulle's method of making this very intricate inlay work is fascinating in itself. Let us suppose they had to veneer two cabinet doors with a half design on each, so the two create a full design. They would glue two sheets of tortoise shell between two sheets of brass of the same thickness, with paper between each sheet, then draw the half design on top and jigsaw the whole sandwich. After cutting they soaked the pieces in water to release the glue. They assembled the pieces so that the background was the tortoise shell and the brass made the design. This was called the Boulle design. But nothing went to waste, so they assembled the left over cut-outs, creating the same design as the first, but reversed, like a photographic negative. Here the background was brass and the design tortoise shell, and they had a second set of doors. This was called counter-Boulle. We are fortunate to have one of the very rare examples, where we can see the two side by side, on these two magnificent pedestals.

There is still a lot of Boulle type furniture around, although there are very few pieces that can be attributed directly to Boulle's workshop. Nevertheless, a great amount of Boulle furniture is being lost every day. The reason for it is that the three materials used — wood, tortoise shell, and brass — (he also used pewter instead of brass on rare occasions) are so completely different that their reactions to changes in temperature and climate are incompatible, with the result that the tortoise shell and brass veneer peel off as the wood shrinks or expands under it. I had the sad task quite a few times of having to strip this veneer from a Boulle piece, which was then refinished in a fruitwood finish because the furniture itself was sound and still in superb condition.

FRENCH, XVIII CENTURY (LOUIS XV)
Finely veneered and
inlaid upright secretary.

The same secretary
with the dropfront open
in writing position,
showing the interior fittings.
The Metropolitan Museum of Art
Anonymous Gift, 1946

FRENCH, LATE XVIII CENTURY (LOUIS XVI)
Beautifully inlaid drop-front secretary with grey marble top.
The Metropolitan Museum of Art   Bequest of Catherine D. Wentworth, 1948

Most of the other furniture of the seventeenth
century was heavily carved, silvered,
or gilded to resemble the metal itself.
The few existing pieces have a beautiful
antique gold glow that the hundreds of years
have left on them. They must have been
quite a sight when they were new,
with the shiny new gold finish on them.
Veneering with exotic and decorative
wood veneers, a technique which was
so widely used by the ancient Egyptians,
Greeks, and Romans, became popular again.

FRENCH, EARLY XVIII CENTURY (LOUIS XV)
Carved archway paneling, the forerunner of the Rococo,
with its partially asymmetrical design.

The Metropolitan Museum of Art
Gift of J. Pierpont Morgan, 1906

All this lasted throughout the
greater part of the seventeenth century.
Early in the eighteenth century
tremendous changes were taking place.
This century has been described
in more glowing terms than any period
during the history of mankind.
The arts and the crafts reached the
crowning glory of achievement. Beauty
and luxury were carried to great extremes,
a sort of last fling before great upheavals
and the advent of the Machine Age
that was to come in the following century.

FRENCH, CA. 1720-1730
Beautifully veneered Regency commode with marble top.

The Metropolitan Museum of Art   Bequest of Catherine D. Wentworth, 1948

During the period known as Règence, furniture
became lighter, more elegant, refined,
and feminine. The leading cabinetmaker of
this period, Charles Cressent, is credited
with developing the Bombé commode.
The French being eternally the same French,
I presume that it was a natural consequence.
After the young Louis XV ascended the throne,
the pursuit of luxury knew no bounds.
Decoration applied to furniture was carried
to great extremes. The bronze work that was
originally intended to protect the furniture
on the corners, around key holes, at the
bottom of the legs, door and drawer pulls,
started to be more elaborate and began
climbing all over the furniture. It was even
used on top of beautiful veneer and inlay work,
culminating in the style known as Rococo.

A top view of this commode,
displaying the same artistic workmanship
and veneering as on the front.
It also has the same inlaid-veneer portrait
panels in the corners as on the front.

Several techniques were used to obtain materials for fine inlaywork such as this. When naturally colorful wood veneers and even stained veneers did not provide sufficient variety of coloring for the design, the craftsman could also add highlights to flowers and leaves by burning part of a leaf or petal. This was done by dipping the veneer into very hot sand or by burning over a candle to the desired shades.

The name is derived from the French word, Rocaille, that simply means rockwork, referring to the rock gardens and imitation grottoes that were in fashion at the time. It was the last word in luxury for one to hide away in his own cave in his backyard. If you think this is odd, considering the luxury some of these people possessed, a noteworthy comparison with today is the people who love to barbecue in the backyard over an open fire, while the kitchen is equipped with electric or even electronic ovens. This is to point to the fact that you do have to examine and judge things in their own environment, circumstances, and context. The Rococo style is also a certain rebellion in itself. Symmetry was (and still is) an unwritten law through the ages in design and decoration. But Rococo threw off the yoke of symmetry and introduced an up-to-then unheard of concept of asymmetry that developed into a fine art. While no two things are alike in a design, it still gives the feeling of unity. The components of this decoration, shells, twigs, leaves, flowers and scrolls, are all different, but instead of pulling apart they harmonize and create one pleasant, even if too elaborate, design. It is interesting to note that the furniture to which this decoration was applied remained always symmetrical and simply elegant, except perhaps for some carved paneling and mirror frames.

After this exuberant Rococo passed its peak of popularity, the Louis XV furniture became more subdued, and a very graceful and elegant style evolved. Chinese lacquer finish, as mentioned before, enjoyed great popularity, and some of the finest pieces made by the greatest of cabinetmakers were finished in Chinese lacquer. Many more-or-less successful attempts were made to duplicate the original Chinese lacquer.

FRENCH, 1790
Drop-front secretary made by Riesener. The shape is familiar to us, but the fantastic inlaywork,
including the Marqueterie a la Reine, is a source of wonder. An unequalled achievement, the epitome of cabinetmaking.
Courtesy of the Frick Collection

Near the middle of the century, the Martin Brothers, who owned three furniture factories, patented a very successful method of lacquering called Vernis Martin, whence the term "Varnish" derives. All other furniture that was not painted or gilded received an oil and wax finish. French polishing, as we know it today, was introduced in the early part of the nineteenth century. About this time archaeological discoveries were taking place in Pompeii and Herculaneum that gave a great impetus toward classical forms in furniture designs. Grecian and Roman architecture had been well known through the ages, but now for the first time people were gaining an insight into the everyday life and the furniture of these ancient people. It was to take some years before furniture would shed its overabundant ormolu and revert to ancient designs.

LOUIS XVI

The style that bears the name of Louis XVI preceded this monarch by a few years, of course without the name being attached to it. The description Neo-Classic fits it perfectly. The trend toward purer classical design based on Grecian and Roman architectural and decorative designs continued, and a graceful elegance emerged in which the decoration was properly subordinate to the design and did not control it.

Furniture making in this latter part of the eighteenth century reached the crowning glory of achievement. The greatest cabinetmakers lived and worked at this time, and created masterpieces. Such high skill was never to be attained again, partly due to the advent of the Machine Age in the early part of the next century. Lumbers used at this time were: next to walnut, mahogany, which gained great popularity, satinwood also came into favor, ebony

was still the last word in luxury, not to mention the numerous exotic woods used for inlaywork. Handwork consisted of sawing the logs into boards and veneer. The logs were seasoned in the yard for months in the sun with the apprentices turning them every few hours so they would dry evenly. After the lengths were cut they were joined and glued to widths required. Then came mortising, dowelling, tongue and grooving, and dovetailing. Most of these operations were required just to put one cabinet together. Then there was shaping of curved cabinet sides and fronts, in the case of serpentine or Bombé front cabinets. Everything was done carefully and skillfully with hand tools, and a lot of pride in a well done job.

Veneering, an art in itself, is a fascinating subject. We shall go into it later in detail, but we should consider here the skill required to overcome the difficult problems arising in veneering, for example, a Bombé shaped front. As we know, wood expands and contracts due to moisture or dryness, in its width only, and veneer gets wet from the glue and tends to shrink and crack if not properly glued. Veneer could be bent only one way at a time, either in the width or in the length, but not both ways at the same time. The effect could be compared to trying to squeeze a piece of flat cardboard on to a half of a ball to make it fit. These are the principal reasons why we have these beautifully set veneers on fronts and side usually of four pieces, with the grain running from the center toward the corner, giving a sort of geometrical sunburst effect. Without being irreverent, one must conclude that the beautiful parquetry work so very popular in the Louis XVI style, especially the "Marqueterie a la Reine" that consists of small flowers within a trellis work, must have been very much favored by the cabinetmakers also. Even though there was much more work involved in cutting and setting up the veneer, gluing and assembly were relatively easier.

FRENCH, 1791 (LOUIS XVI)
Riesener made this commode a year after the secretary, obviously to match it.
His signature and date appear in the lower right hand corner of the center panel in each cabinet.
Courtesy of the Frick Collection

Another type of parquetry also was very popular. Geometric patterns of contrasting woods created remarkable three-dimensional illusions. The Ebeniste let his imagination run wild, experimenting with the limitless variation in repetitive forms and tonal values. Instead of the Espagnoletta or "Spanish Woman" busts which had been popular in the past for use as corner ormolues, fluted or reeded columns came into fashion.

The fluted style contained husks or quills on the top and bottom of the fluting, leaving the middle unadorned. The reeded column usually had a gilded ribbon carved on it, giving the appearance of a sheaf of reeds tied about with ribbons. Legs were also fluted or reeded and tapered. Sèvres porcelain plaques were used to a great extent, surrounded usually by green gilded ormolu. This color effect was achieved by mixing silver with the gold used for gilding.

This simple form of geometric parquetry giving a three dimensional impression was an innovation of J. F. Oeben.

From the Author's workshop. Made by A. Sztrykler

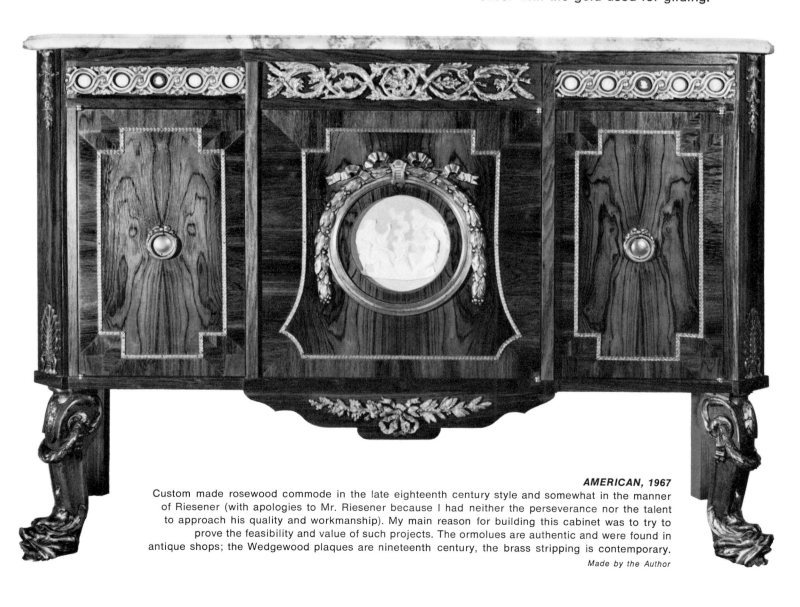

AMERICAN, 1967

Custom made rosewood commode in the late eighteenth century style and somewhat in the manner of Riesener (with apologies to Mr. Riesener because I had neither the perseverance nor the talent to approach his quality and workmanship). My main reason for building this cabinet was to try to prove the feasibility and value of such projects. The ormolues are authentic and were found in antique shops; the Wedgewood plaques are nineteenth century, the brass stripping is contemporary.

Made by the Author

Louis XVI was a fine locksmith
and created many original locks himself.
In those days all locks were made by hand
and lockmaking was an art in itself.
His favorite place was in his workshop.
Queen Marie Antoinette preferred to work
in the garden or in the dairy barn than suffer
the pomp and splendor of a sterile society.
However, she did spend great fortunes
on furniture. For that we shall be thankful,
for we have the privilege and the pleasure
of seeing the masterpieces of an epoch
where handwork was in its reigning glory,
amidst a decaying pompous society
that was to be swept away by revolution.
Maybe it is one of the injustices of history
that the king to suffer the consequences
was the one who admired and respected
the craftsman and the worker the most.
This magnificent furniture of a
magnificent age reached a peak
of perfection never again achieved.

FRENCH, XVIII CENTURY
Examples of ormolu.

The Metropolitan Museum of Art
Gift of J. Pierpont Morgan, 1906

Following this great upheaval there were several less important short periods of furniture styles named after the ruling governments which held power in France: the Directoire; the Revolutionary Government; the Consulate; Napoleon's government before he became Emperor; and, of course, the dazzling Empire. What the first two lack in elegance, imagination and glitter, the Empire style makes up for. With Napoleon's ascension to the throne, new and radically different influences in design were prominently displayed in furniture. Cabinetmakers, who were traditionally dependent on France as a source of inspiration, were caught up in the archeological excitement and innovation caused by Napoleon's adventure in the Mediterranean and the wealth of souvenirs he brought back to France.

FRENCH, 1785-1790
Secretary, matching piece
(en suite) to the commode.
It must have been made at the same time
for the Queen Marie Antoinette.
The ormolu mounts for these two pieces
were made by Pierre Gouthiere (1732-1813).
The Metropolitan Museum of Art
Bequest of William K. Vanderbilt, 1920

The Queen's monogram.

The secretary, open,
reveals the superb interior
fittings. You may notice
that some of the drawers
do not fit properly.
We may attribute this
to the fact that this piece
is over 180 years old.

A glorifying splendor appeared in furniture,
based mostly on Egyptian and Grecian
motifs. Sphinxes, winged lions, swans, eagles
and other fanciful creatures abounded
in meaningless and often overwhelming
profusion. Most of these themes had been
used before, but not to this extent.
Everything that was previously held in high
esteem, including quality and workmanship,
was discarded in disfavor. There was little
or no demand for exquisite craftsmanship and
superior design, as the new establishment
did not follow the past tradition of
sponsoring the arts and crafts.
The art of furniture making declined in France.

ANDRE-CHARLES BOULLE (1642-1732)

One of the most famous and celebrated cabinetmakers, Boulle was born in Paris, the son of a very artistic cabinetmaker. He showed great promise at an early age and by the time he was thirty years old Louis XIV named him the "first cabinetmaker to the Court," with a workshop in the Louvre. As such, he was free of the restrictions of the Guild and could work with bronze and

FRENCH, XVIII CENTURY
A magnificent Louis XIV commode, made by a cabinetmaker who must have been a great admirer of Boulle. In this piece he faithfully copied the tiniest detail of Boulle's great commodes. Boulle made four identical commodes similar to this one, and, from among the hundreds of pieces he made during his long career, the commodes are the only four pieces which can be attributed to Boulle with certainty.
Courtesy of the Frick Collection

FRENCH, CA. 1780-1790
Arm chair made by Sulpice Brizard.
It is always the mark of good craftsmanship
when the twistings face each other,
as it is done on these legs,
left and right hand spirals, respectively.

The Metropolitan Museum of Art
Gift of George Blumenthal, 1941

other metals. (Cabinetmakers, in general, were prohibited from working in metals.) Boulle employed about twenty master cabinetmakers, also some of the finest bronze workers, and designed and produced a great amount of furniture. His fame spread all over the world. Kings, princes, and anyone who could afford to pay fortunes, vied with each other for his furniture. In spite of his great success Boulle was continuously faced with financial problems, in part because most of his customers were tardy payers, and partly due to his own prodigal nature. He continuously bought art treasures at great expense, even buying back his own work, often paying much more than he had sold it for. In 1720, when he was 78 years old, a great disaster struck him. His workshop burned down and he lost everything he owned. Disregarding his advanced age, with great ambition and energy he reestablished his position as the leading cabinetmaker of the time and founded a dynasty of highly regarded cabinetmakers. Four of his sons followed in his footsteps. Each bore the title "Cabinetmaker to the King."

JEAN-BAPTISTE BOULARD (ca. 1725-1789)

Boulard achieved fame quite late in his life after Louis XVI ordered furniture from him which he made with great skill and ability. He worked in both Louis XV and Louis XVI styles, but he excelled in the latter with very beautiful chairs and small tables.

SULPICE BRIZARD (c. 1735-1798)

Brizard acquired his Master's degree in 1762. Three years later he opened his own workshop where he produced chairs of very high quality. He was one of the main suppliers of chairs and other seating furniture to the Court of Louis XVI in the early years of his reign. Brizard had a brother, Pierre, who was also a master craftsman with his own workshop.

MARTIN CARLIN (? -1785)

In spite of his French name, Martin Carlin was
of German extraction, the son of a carpenter
of Freiburg-Im Breisgau. He arrived in Paris
in 1759 and went to work for J. F. Oeben,
which, in itself, was quite an accomplishment.
Soon after, he married Oeben's younger sister.
Carlin's good friend, Roger Vandercruse, who
was Mrs. Oeben's brother, may have helped to
bring about this marriage. Carlin became
a Master in 1766, and established his own
workshop where he produced furniture of very
high quality and beauty. Sèvres porcelain
plaques, marble mosaics, ormolu, and
very skillful veneer inlaywork mark
his luxurious and dignified furniture.

CHARLES CRESSENT (1685-1768)

Cressent came from a family of cabinetmakers;
both his grandfather and father were well
known craftsmen. Charles served apprenticeship
in his father's workshop. After becoming
a master craftsman, he went to work for
Joseph Paitou, a competitor of Boulle.
Later he married Paitou's widow and
took charge of the workshop. The Regent,
Duc Philippe d'Orleans, recognized his great
talent and artistry, and named him his first
cabinetmaker. As mentioned before, he is
credited with developing the Bombé commode.

MATHIEU CRIAERD (1689-1776)

The Flemish Criaerd family of cabinetmakers
had a number of master craftsmen members.
Mathieu received his Master's degree in 1738,
and practiced his trade with great success.
Before he established his own workshop,
he worked for the very famous J. F. Oeben,
which was practically a guarantee to fame
in those days. His work was of very high quality:
extremely fine inlaywork, Chinese lacquer,
and highly polished furniture fitted
with beautiful bronzes. Indeed — elegant!

PIERRE-ANTOINE FOULLET (?-1775)

Foullet became a Master cabinetmaker in 1749.
He is best known as the creator of fine
clockcases, especially because he produced a
great many of them. However, the furniture
he made also ranks with the best in
quality, in workmanship and in elegance.
The magnificent inlaywork he produced is
composed of a great variety of wood veneers.

GEORGES JACOB (1739-1814)

Georges, one of the most famous chairmakers, was born of a peasant family. His success as a cabinetmaker was exceptional in an age of close knit family ownership of the workshop, when certain trade "secrets" were kept as zealously guarded family treasures. The trade was taught to the family members, first and foremost. What with the Guilds, breaking into the art of cabinetmaking was no mean feat in itself. The achievement required a very clever and talented young man.

Georges served his apprenticeship in the workshop of the famed Delanois. He became Master in 1765.

The "Chef d'Ouvre," his masterpiece which he submitted to the Guild, a model of an arm chair, won him his Master's degree. (It is still in the possession of his descendants.) He established his own workshop and was an instant success. His reputation soon spread and orders poured in from all over Europe. Georges' very good friend, the famous painter Jean-Louis David, designed and ordered chairs from him in the Etruscan, Grecian, and Roman styles which he used in his paintings.

The most famous chaise longue in history, the one on which Madame Récamier posed for her portrait by David, was fashioned by Georges, and that classical style is known as Récamier. Georges used very dark mahogany to resemble old bronze. Many of his pieces were the predecessors of the future Empire style.

His chairs show a remarkable quality, fine proportions, with carving so crisp and deep, it appears as though it were pierced through. After retiring in 1796, he gave his workshop to his sons, who followed in the same tradition.

ENGLISH XVIII CENTURY
Finely carved and gilded armchair made by Ince and Mayhew for
Croome Court.

The Metropolitan Museum of Art, Gift of the
Samuel H. Kress Foundation, 1958

FRENCH LATE
XVIII EARLY XIX CENTURY
Rosewood Veneered Pier table, made by Charles Honore Lannuier.
The Brooklyn Museum, Gift of the Pierrepen Family

FRENCH, XVIII CENTURY
Veneered and inlaid tambour-front table, made by Lacroix.
Apparently the beautiful inlaywork that contained
veneers stained in different colors has faded.
Nevertheless, the skill of the craftsman is evident.

The Metropolitan Museum of Art   Bequest of Mary Stillman Harkness, 1948

FRENCH, 1769
Exquisite Louis XVI commode, made by Lacroix,
attests to his superb craftsmanship.

Courtesy of The Frick Collection

Roger Vandercruse Lacroix's signature, *R.V.L.C. JME.*
One of the most highly respected stamps in furniture
because of his impeccable workmanship,
but with all those brothers-in-law around, he'd better.

The Metropolitan Museum of Art
Bequest of Mary Stillman Harkness, 1948

ROGER VANDERCRUSE-LACROIX (1728-1799)

Roger Lacroix was a great cabinetmaker
of Flemish descent. He was born in Paris
where the family took on the name of Lacroix.
He became a master in 1755, and took over
his father's workshop, which he managed
with success. Lacroix was a high official of
the cabinetmakers' Guild for many years.
He had a brother who was a famous
clockmaker, and five sisters, three of whom
married the most celebrated cabinetmakers
of the time: J. F. Oeben, his brother Simon,
and Simon Guillaume. They certainly
believed in keeping it in the family. Roger's
furniture excels in refined workmanship.

FRENCH, 1780-1790
Leleu made this very elegant table (bureau plat) decorated with painted Sèvres porcelain plaques, ormolu and inlaid veneer work.

The Metropolitan Museum of Art   The Jules S. Bache Collection, 1949

JEAN-FRANCOIS LELEU (1729-1807)

Leleu is one of the very few who did not come from a family of cabinetmakers, but started out as a plain laborer. After apprenticeship, he was accepted and hired by the famous J. F. Oeben. Leleu worked there at the same time as another great cabinetmaker, Riesener. They were both top workers and vied with each other for advancement, and later on for the possession of Oeben's workshop. However, Riesener succeeded and won both the workshop and the widow Oeben's hand in marriage. Leleu, one of the few Frenchmen among the top cabinetmakers during the reign of Louis XVI, continued working for Riesener for a while. But he probably bore a mean grudge against Riesener because of his own defeats by Riesener's superior skill as a craftsman and his ability to charm the boss lady. Leleu was a man of quick temper (as police records show), and "he knocked Riesener on the head several times, and threw his hat in the mud," after which he set up his own workshop. Leleu was very successful, in spite of the fact that the courts favored Riesener's and Benneman's work over his.

JEAN-FRANCOIS OEBEN (c. 1720-1763)

"One of the greatest of the greats" was said to describe Jean-Francois Oeben. In his short lifetime, he achieved what few of the great artisans ever accomplished. Of German origin, as were many of the cabinetmakers who worked in Paris at that time, Oeben made a name for himself at an early age. After his marriage to Miss Vandercruse, the sister of Roger Vandercruse-Lacroix, Oeben went to work for Charles-Joseph Boulle, the son of the great Andre-Charles Boulle. In 1754, Oeben received the title "Cabinetmaker to the King," and with it a house and a workshop at Gobelins. He was also granted special permission to make mechanical devices for the furniture he made at which he was very adept. Oeben had the good sense to surround himself with some of the greatest craftsmen of the time. In 1760, he received an order to build a desk for the King. This, the most famous desk

in the history of furniture, was filled
with mechanical contrivances. It soon proved
to be a monumental task, and Oeben worked on
it the last three years of his life, not
exclusively, we may safely assume. His heir,
Riesener, worked on it another six years.
It turned out to be one of the masterpieces
of the great age of cabinetmaking.

JEAN-HENRY RIESENER (1734-1806)

If all of the above and below mentioned
cabinetmakers are deserving of the superlatives:
The Great, One of the Greatest, and so on,
Riesener deserves to be called THE Greatest.
He reached the epitome of the art
of woodworking, a height of skill no one
ever before or after him achieved.
He was also of German extraction, born at
Gladbeck near Essen. Riesener, as a very
young man, went to work for Oeben
and probably served his apprenticeship there.

FRENCH, 1774
This splendid commode was made by J. H. Riesener
in 1774 as a temporary furnishing for Louis XVI's bedroom.
Said Riesener, "This will have to do until I can make a better one."

As mentioned previously, in 1763
Riesener was granted the
management of Oeben's workshop.
He received his Master's degree in 1768,
and from then on he used his own
stamp on all the furniture he made.
Riesener's furniture was always
successful in beauty, in proportions,
and excellent workmanship. The trapezoid
center panel is one of his innovations.
Some of his masterpieces
were made for Marie Antoinette,
her monogram worked in the center
of the frieze, inside a wreath.
One of the most famous pieces of furniture
which Riesener worked on, undoubtedly,
would be the aforementioned "King's Desk"
that took him six years to finish.
Truly a great artisan.

FRENCH, CA. 1795
The most magnificent piece
of cabinetwork in existence.
This jewel cabinet was made by J. H. Riesener
for the Comtesse of Provence,
Louis XVI's sister-in-law.
The jewel-like quality
of the gilded bronze mounts
is in keeping with the
excellence of the woodworking.
It has been assumed that these
superb ormolu were made by Gouthiere,
but that is not proven.
This cabinet was offered for sale
by a Madame Aulmont to Napoleon
when he became emperor,
and she received the answer that
"His Highness prefers to have new furniture made."
Jacob Desmalter, a famous cabinetmaker
of the time, made a pair of similar
but cheaper versions of this piece.
In 1825 this cabinet was bought
for 420 pounds for King George IV.
One of the finest masterpieces
of the greatest craftsman
of the eighteenth century,
it has remained since then
in the English Royal Collection.

Approximately 4'6" wide and 9' high.
Crown Copyright Reserved

The cresting shows cherubim placing the fleur-de-lis crown on the coat of arms of France and Savoy.

The open doors reveal eighteen drawers, shelves, the paneled back.
The lock is also noteworthy. (Locks were also custom-made to each cabinet.)
It locks the left door with three tongues and also the top and the bottom of the right door.
There are additional drawers in the frieze and in the apron.

In the bronze mounts on the two center doors
are the symbols of married happiness:
the harp, the doves, garlands and Cupid's arrows.

The minute detail
of the exquisite bronze work
adds greatly to
the charm of this cabinet.

FRENCH, LATE XVIII CENTURY

A superb roll-top desk made by J. H. Riesener
for Louis XVI. It closely resembles the celebrated
desk made for Louis XV that his predecessor,
J. F. Oeben, started and he finished, but this one
has the trapezoid shaped center panel and
the Marqueterie a la Reine (waterlilies set within
a trelliswork in inlaid veneer), both Riesener's
innovations. As expected of Riesener's work,
everything about it is beauty and perfection:
the construction, the veneering, finishing,
the gilded bronze work that he designed,
specified and ordered from a bronzemaker.
All these things in harmony make up a masterpiece
such as this magnificent desk.

The desk open displays
stationery drawers, shelves
and green leather writing surface.

A view from the top shows palm leaf ormolu terminating in candlesticks (a very important feature before electricity). The beautifully veneered cylinder top is cut into wide slats to roll like a tambour door, and so skillfully done that it is hardly noticeable.

The back detail shows beautiful floral marquetry work.

Enlarged view of cylinder front.

Initials D.R. intertwined, are set into the block
under the keyhole escutcheon in the center drawer.

The Roentgen desk open reveals stationery drawers,
a pullout writing surface, file drawers and secret compartments.

DAVID ROENTGEN (1743-1807)

Roentgen, also an internationally known
cabinetmaker, was born in Neuwied, Germany,
where his father, Abraham Roentgen,
had his cabinetmaking workshop.
David served his apprenticeship
there, and in 1772 took charge
of the already well known workshop.
Under his management, the shop flourished.
He employed about one hundred
master craftsmen and they turned out
huge quantities of high quality furniture
for the heads of states and the
wealthy of Europe, including,
of course, Louis XVI and his court.
Roentgen opened a showroom in Paris
where the furniture built at Neuwied
was sold. The demand was so great that he
was compelled to open a workshop there,
after passing his Master's test in 1780.
Roentgen's furniture was very much favored
because it usually included ingenious
mechanical devices and very fine workmanship.
Roentgen developed an extremely hard
and lustrous finish on his beautiful
furniture. (The process is unknown today.)
He never stamped his furniture, but he
worked his monogram into the inlaywork.
sometimes unobtrusively, but occasionally
displayed quite obviously.

FRENCH, CA. 1775-1780
Cylinder top desk by David Roentgen.
Veneered with magnificent inlaywork of Chinese scenes, satinwood cross-banding
veneerwork also contains walnut burl, sycamore, tulipwood, ebony and greenheart.

The Metropolitan Museum of Art
Rogers Fund, 1941

FRENCH, CA. 1780
Cylinder top desk made by David Roentgen.
Fine workmanship makes his work
outstanding among furniture treasures.

The Metropolitan Museum of Art
Gift of The Samuel H. Kress Foundation, 1958

FRENCH, CA. 1765 (lower right)
This fine table was made by Bernard Van Risen Burgh
and bears his stamp B.V.R.B.
It is finished with
green Vernis Martin, "Varnish" finish.

The Metropolitan Museum of Art
Gift of The Samuel H. Kress Foundation, 1958

BERNARD VAN RISEN BURGH

B.V.R.B.

These are the most famous initials
in the history of cabinetmaking.
Until very recently, mystery surrounded
the identity of the producer of the
superb and exceptionally high quality
furniture signed with these initials.
It was pure speculation as to whom they
represented until the famed French scholar,
Jean-Pierre Baroli, after long research,
discovered a piece of paper in the archives
identifying this great cabinetmaker.
Actually, there were three generations
of cabinetmakers with the same name.
The first Bernard arrived in Paris
about the end of the seventeenth century
and became a Master craftsman in 1722.
He worked in the popular Boulle style
and never signed his work.
His son, the second Bernard, is the one who
signed the furniture he made with the
famed and long unrecognized initials.
He became Master about 1730 and created the
exquisite furniture that gave him his fame.
The third Bernard, his son, no less
an artisan than his father or grandfather,
never passed the Master's test, and so,
when the workshop was left to him,
he had to give it up and went to
work as a sculptor and woodcarver.

FRENCH, XVIII CENTURY

One of a set of magnificent arm chairs made by
Sene and bearing his stamp, as shown at right.
After about two hundred years of use their
condition is still as excellent as if
they had been made recently.

Collection of Mr. & Mrs. Gerald Bregman, New York City
Photograph by the Author

JEAN-BAPTISTE-CLAUDE SENE (1748-1803)

Sene was born into a family whose
many members, father and forefathers,
were cabinetmakers. He passed his Master's
test at the unusually early age of twenty-one.
Soon after he established himself in his own
workshop where he produced great quantities
of furniture for private customers, and
for the Furniture Warehouse Administration.
Shortly before the Revolution, he built a throne
for the King's conference room in the palace.
Sene was one of the few cabinetmakers who
continued in favor after the Revolution.
At one time, he received an order for
two hundred desks for officials
of the Revolutionary government.

FRENCH, CA. 1788

Daybed (lit de repos), carved of walnut, painted and gilded.
Made for Marie Antoinette by Sené.
The feature by which some of his work may be identified
are the legs which terminate on top with Ionic capitals.
Superb craftsmanship places his achievements
among the treasures of the furniture world.

The Metropolitan Museum of Art
Gift of Ann Payne Blumenthal, 1941

FRENCH, MID XVIII CENTURY
Slant top desk, beautifully shaped
and veneered with fine inlaywork.
Made by Jean-Baptiste Tuart,
who became a Master in 1741.

The Metropolitan Museum of Art
Bequest of Collis P. Huntington, 1926

FRENCH, CA. 1760
A very skillfully veneered and inlaid commode, made with tulipwood,
harewood, and various other woods. The cabinetmaker is unknown.

The Metropolitan Museum of Art   The Jules S. Bache Collection, 1949

FRENCH, CA. 1790
Very elegant upright secretary
made by Adam Weisweiler.
The large Sèvres painted porcelain panel
in the center of the door is flanked by
Wedgwood medallions on either side.

The Metropolitan Museum of Art
Gift of The Samuel H. Kress Foundation, 1958

JEAN-BAPTISTE TILLIARD (1685-1776)

Tilliard was born into a family of cabinetmakers,
and like many cabinetmakers of the time,
learned the trade in the family workshop.
He became famous after making furniture for
Versailles. Tilliard chairs are especially
noteworthy in that he is credited with
changing the position of chair arms,
which previously started above the front legs,
moving them further back to accommodate
panniers, the wire framework that the ladies
used to wear under their skirts.

ADAM WEISWEILER (c. 1750-1809)

Weisweiler, a fellow countryman (Landsman)
of Roentgen, was also born in Neuwied
and probably served his apprenticeship
in the Roentgen workshop. He went to Paris
and received his Master's degree in 1778.
After that he established his own workshop
where he made unusually elegant and luxurious
furniture in pure Louis XVI style.
Sèvres porcelain plaques, pietra dura
(hard stone) inlaywork, and ebony veneering
mark his fine work. A very distinctive
feature of his furniture is the intertwined
stretcher connecting the legs together.

FRENCH, XVIII CENTURY

Armoire, made of oak in the Louis XV style.
This style, without as much carving,
became very popular and widespread.
It is known today as French Provincial.

*The Metropolitan Museum of Art
Gift of J. Pierpont Morgan, 1906*

FRENCH PROVINCIAL — *Of all the furniture styles made by the French cabinetmakers, the most honest one, if the term may be applied to furniture, is the French Provincial. From the time of Louis XIV on, the majority of the people of France, in the provinces and cities, embraced a furniture style that is both beautiful and functional in other words, furniture to live with. It is fine to have those great art treasures of furniture decorating palaces and the homes of the rich and sophisticated in society, but who would want or even dare to put his dirty socks in the drawer of a commode made by Riesener, for example. French Provincial covers a large area of furniture decoration, and it can always be recognized as such. It is always functional and decorative, and almost always the wood itself is left to show its richness, hardly ever painted. In addition, the shaping and carving enhance this style of furniture. For these reasons, it has enjoyed a great popularity.*

ENGLISH, CA. 1475
Oak cupboard
with pierced Gothic design
is of peg and groove
construction, and was used
for storage of food.
*The Metropolitan Museum of Art
Rogers Fund, 1910*

Enlarged view of pierced
quatrefoil. Its bold simplicity is
remarkably like the
stone carving of the period.

ENGLAND

The art of furniture making was undoubtedly
introduced by the Romans during their
occupation of England from 55 B.C.
to 407 A.D. which is quite a long time
by any measure. The Romans were known for
imposing their culture and mode of living on
subjugated countries. We know this fact from
the struggles of small nations who would not
comply with the imposed culture and religion.
However, that is another story for another
day, and it suffices to say that the Roman
influence on furnishing disappeared so
completely that there is no trace of it today.
When the early English people discarded the
lavish and luxurious Roman style of furniture,
the way it was made was also forgotten.

Cabinetmaking reverted to the primitive and the English started out from the very beginning again. Scooped out tree trunks served as storage chests, furniture evolved slowly, and in the early Middle Ages most household furnishings consisted of rough-hewn chests, benches, and trestle tables. Cupboards, which meant just that, boards or shelves fastened to the wall to hold cups and dishes, eventually became cabinets as we know them today.

The English home contained one large hall (heal) which served as dining, living and sleeping room. In the center of this hall was the hearth, which was used for heating and cooking. The smoke escaped through a louvre in the roof. There was a room next to the hall called the Bower, or Chamber, reserved strictly for the ladies of the household (admirable custom). Here they did their weaving, sewing, and spinning — more than one yarn, to be sure. This may be the room that became the parloir, later called the parlor. Talking room?

When the hall was used for dining, two tables were set up on sawhorses in a "T" shape. The floor was one step (about one foot) higher at one end of the hall where the table forming the top of the "T" was set, for the Lord, his family, and noble guests. The table forming the leg of the "T" was set on the lower floor for the employees and other rankless guests. The dish of salt, a very important item at those meals, was placed where the two tables joined; hence the status measuring expressions, above the salt, and below the salt.

Needless to say, in the huts and cottages of the common folk these problems did not exist. Floors were simply stomped-down earth mixed with lime, strewn with rush or straw that was never removed, but rather covered by new rush and fragrant leaves spread over the old when it was crushed and mushy.

The bed, that started out as a large straw-filled sack on the floor in one corner, eventually received a platform with legs to lift it off that drafty cold floor. It was then moved to its own room where it became the main feature with a very elaborate canopy supported by turned and carved posts and headboard.

Against this background the cabinetmaker of the Middle Ages worked, using the fine timber of the English countryside: oak, ash, elm, pine and fruitwoods, such as apple, pear, cherry, and so on. Walnut, which was originally brought to England by the Romans, was scarce until late in the Elizabethan era. Queen Elizabeth had many walnut trees planted in the early years of her reign. Walnut trees need 40 to 50 years to reach maturity, so the Queen actually saw furniture made from the trees she caused to be planted. Following this, walnut furniture was in such great demand that the period after her reign became known as the Age of Walnut, and the time prior to it the Age of Oak. Mahogany was not used by English cabinetmakers until the early part of the 18th century.

How about the method of working? If one could afford the luxury of mysticism, he might say that some kind of spirit of cabinetmaking went around the world, teaching the skills of the trade in every country. This would make things very simple and easy to understand, but not nearly as interesting. The early English craftsman started out literally from scratch, just as had his Egyptian ancestor four thousand years before. He made dugout tree trunks, as mentioned above, to serve as storage chests. They evolved into chests made of planks with butt joined nailed corners, then reinforced with straps, and later into sophisticated dovetailed chests. Grooving, glueing, mortise and tenoning gradually developed parallel to one another and on the same principles as in ancient times.

To what can we credit the remarkable similarity in development of this art that stretched from Egypt to China, encompassing the whole civilized world? One may come to the conclusion that furniture is a natural development in evolution, and for the well being of mankind. Very much like language or clothing, it may differ in style from country to country, but it all springs from the same principle, for the same purpose, serving the same universal need. We must conclude that the art of woodworking is a natural development. Slowly but surely the English cabinetmakers reached superb levels of accomplishment just as the French, Dutch, and other highly skilled craftsmen did, and his workmanship takes second place to none.

ENGLISH, LATE XVI CENTURY

A canopied bed made of oak and inlaid with walnut and ebony. The posters are turned and carved out of ash boles (tree trunks).
The headboard is paneled with moldings and carvings. From Cumnor Palace, Berkshire, England.
The Metropolitan Museum of Art Gift of Irwin Untermyer, 1953.

ENGLISH, CA. 1720-1730
Side table of mahogany. The top is inlaid with a symmetrical strapwork or ribbon. It has cabriole legs with pad feet.
Courtesy Victoria and Albert Museum

The Renaissance knocked at England's door too, awakening the arts and crafts to new things, new ideas, and a new mode of living. When Henry VIII came to the throne, America had just recently been discovered, the stir of a new awareness was sweeping the country. He had the None-Such Palace built to surpass all palaces on the continent of Europe, in architecture and in furnishing. Sadly enough, it does not exist today. Another great impetus was given by Queen Elizabeth, under whose intellectual leadership furniture started to take on the typical English look which it retained throughout all foreign styles and influences.

ENGLISH, CA. 1600
Draw table made of oak. The apron is inlaid with sycamore, bog oak and other woods. The heavy vase shaped legs have Ionic capitals.
Courtesy Victoria and Albert Museum

106

ENGLISH, CA. 1690
Table made of walnut and walnut veneer
with seaweed marquetry, Boulle style.
Veneered cabriole legs, joined by
a veneered and inlaid stretcher,
and supported on bun feet.
*The Metropolitan Museum of Art
Collection of Irwin Untermyer*

There were many important,
and some less important phases of
English furniture making, each worthy
of extensive description and explanation.
For our purpose, a chronology should suffice.
If truly, one picture is worth a thousand words,
let us study and visually enjoy the handwork
displayed in the following photographs of
the best known works by English cabinetmakers.

ENGLISH, EARLY XIX CENTURY
An unusually beautiful round table with a
concave tripod base (monopodium)
with lion's paw feet. Mahogany,
inlaid with ebony and silver.
Designed by Thomas Hope, a famed
designer of classical style furniture,
for his own house at Deepdene.
Courtesy Victoria and Albert Museum

ENGLISH CABINETMAKERS — *The lives and works of the English cabinetmakers are far less well documented than the French cabinetmakers, who were registered with the Guilds and signed and sometimes also dated their work. The scant knowledge was compiled from old newspaper advertising, directories, memoirs, invoices, and very rarely, from their labels that were pasted inside the cabinets. Very few are in existence today. In spite of this peculiarity, the English cabinetmaker, as said before, takes second place to none. The names of some are practically household words the world over, and their works are highly regarded art treasures.*

ENGLISH, XVIII CENTURY
One of the few pieces of furniture that can be attributed with certainty to Thomas Chippendale is this magnificent breakfront bookcase that testifies to his great artistry as a cabinetmaker. With Rococo style carvings, it is an English masterpiece. The enlarged detail shows the excellent skill and workmanship of Chippendale. The veneering, inlaywork, moldings and carving are of the best quality and beautiful proportions.
By Permission of the Earl of Pembroke

ROBERT ADAM (1728-1792)

Robert Adam was not a cabinetmaker. He was an architect and furniture designer, but his name comes up so often when 18th century English furniture is mentioned that he should be admitted to this august group. Adam designed in the neo-classical style, using satinwood, painted-on designs and paintings in round or oval frames. The most famous painter who decorated Adam style furniture was Angelica Kauffmann. Her work was copied on Adam style furniture as long as the style lasted. Thomas Chippendale made many of the pieces designed by Adam.

THOMAS CHIPPENDALE (1718-1779)

Thomas Chippendale came from a family of woodworkers, as his forbears had been carpenters and cabinetmakers for generations. His father was a chairmaker. Chippendale was a very talented craftsman at an early age. Judging from the furniture ascribed to him, he certainly defied the notion that his only claim to fame was the publication of his book "The Gentleman & Cabinetmaker's Director" which appeared in 1754 when he was only thirty-six years old. It may have helped to call attention to his great artistry as a cabinetmaker. The book brought fame on its own merit, however, and so did the very high quality of the furniture he made. This made him a legend in his own lifetime, and possibly forever.

ENGLISH, XVIII CENTURY
Another breakfront bookcase made by Chippendale,
showing the same pediment on top,
the star inlaywork, and moldings on
the lower doors as on the previous one.
By Permission of the Earl of Pembroke

ENGLISH, XIX CENTURY
Pot Table (pronounced "poe"), an Empire style cabinet,
served as a pre-plumbing bedroom accessory.
Usually fluted and veneered with mahogany,
walnut, or rosewood, with a semi-concealed
door and marble top in a wood frame,
it was supposed to look like a columnar pedestal
for a statue, or better, a vase with fragrant flowers.
Reproduced in the Author's Workshop

ENGLISH, 1765-1775
Chippendale mahogany chair with ladder-back.
The Metropolitan Museum of Art   Rogers Fund, 1908

IRISH, CA. 1730
Chippendale side table.
Fine but massively carved, of mahogany.
*The Metropolitan Museum of Art
Bequest of John L. Cadwalader, 1914*

ENGLISH, LATE XVII CENTURY
A side table of walnut
with marquetry decoration
and twisted legs.
Courtesy Victoria and Albert Museum

Top view shows elaborate inlaywork.

ENGLISH, LATE XVIII CENTURY
Side table, painted and decorated in the Adam style.
The legs are fluted, carved and gilded.
Courtesy Victoria and Albert Museum

ENGLISH, EARLY XVIII CENTURY
Grandfather clock made of oak and walnut,
inlaid with various woods,
of the Queen Anne period.
Movement made by Joseph Windmills.
The Metropolitan Museum of Art
Bequest of William Mitchell, 1922

ENGLISH, CA. 1690
Highly carved walnut chair
of the William and Mary period.
It is notable for its cartouche shaped,
pierced and carved back,
shaped stretchers with a central finial,
and turned and carved legs
that terminate in paw feet.
The Metropolitan Museum of Art
Collection of Irwin Untermyer

SAMUEL BENNETT

Samuel Bennett, a fine cabinetmaker, worked in
London during the latter part of the 17th century.

JOHN BOROUGHS

John Boroughs was appointed cabinetmaker to
Charles II, and later to William and Mary.

JOHN BRADBURN

John Bradburn, a master cabinetmaker,
made furniture for the royal palaces,
from about 1765. Before that, he was
employed by the firm of Vile and Cobb.

ENGLISH, CA. 1755
Detail of the back of a side chair. This is called a ribband back because the carving depicts ribbon tied into a bow in the center. Hanging tassels are carved into the uprights.
A magnificent example of fine cabinetwork and carving.

The Metropolitan Museum of Art   Collection of Irwin Untermyer

ENGLISH, CA. 1760-1770
Fine serpentine front commode,
inlaid with floral marquetry, with gilded mounts applied.

The Metropolitan Museum of Art   Fletcher Fund, 1959

The Firm of G. COXED and T. WOSTER

Coxed and Woster were famous cabinetmakers. Some of their work is notable for the stained elm burl veneering and inlay of pewter.

ROBERT GILLOW (1703-1773)

Robert Gillow, a very successful cabinetmaker, exported much of his furniture to America.

GILES GRENDEY (1693-1780)

Giles Grendey was a well known cabinetmaker and chairmaker of his time. He made and exported furniture to Spain and Portugal.

ENGLISH, CA. 1755-1760
Chair of carved mahogany in the
"Chinese Chippendale" style.
The fretwork carved into the aprons
and legs is especially beautiful.
Courtesy Victoria and Albert Museum

ENGLISH, CA. 1755
Mahogany and mahogany veneer bureau cabinet
in the "Chinese Chippendale" style.
Its features are the pagoda top
and applied molding tracery.
*The Metropolitan Museum of Art
Collection of Irwin Untermyer*

ENGLISH, CA. 1750
"Chinese Chippendale" arm chair,
painted white; relief and decoration gilded.
The Metropolitan Museum of Art   Rogers Fund, 1931

As we know, the Chinese vogue
swept all over Europe in the mid-eighteenth
century, manifesting itself among cabinetmakers
in the wide use of Chinese lacquered panels and
furniture. Thomas Chippendale designed and
made a whole line of "Chinese" style furniture
which even the Chinese had not yet thought of.

ENGLISH, CA. 1677-1680
Architectural woodwork. Beautiful, richly carved banister and staircase,
made of pine, ash, and oak. Built by Grinling Gibbons.
Previously at Cassiobury Park, Watford, Hertfordshire.
The Metropolitan Museum of Art
Rogers Fund, 1932

GRINLING GIBBONS (1648-1720)
Grinling Gibbons was a great cabinetmaker,
master carpenter, and carver, his work
was always monumental and excellent.

THOMAS HAIG

Thomas Haig, an excellent cabinetmaker,
was a partner of both the elder
and younger Thomas Chippendale.

GERREIT JENSEN

Gerreit Jensen was the famed cabinetmaker
to the Crown, from about 1680-1714. He made
furniture in the popular "Boulle" style.

PETER LANGLOIS

Peter Langlois was a French cabinetmaker
who worked in London. He was also well
known for his fine "Boulle" style furniture.

ABRAHAM ROENTGEN (1711-1793)

Abraham Roentgen was a very famous German
cabinetmaker. He was the father of David
Roentgen, who is mentioned among the French
cabinetmakers. Abraham worked in England
from about 1731 to 1738. He was a highly
skilled craftsman. He attempted to emigrate
to America, but was shipwrecked near Ireland.
After that, he returned to Germany, where
he established the workshop which, through
father and son, became world renowned.

AMERICAN, CA. 1790-1795
Hepplewhite bookcase secretary.
Fine mahogany veneering and inlaywork.
From Baltimore, Maryland.
The Metropolitan Museum of Art
Gift of the Members of the Committee of the Bertha King Benkard Memorial Fund, 1946

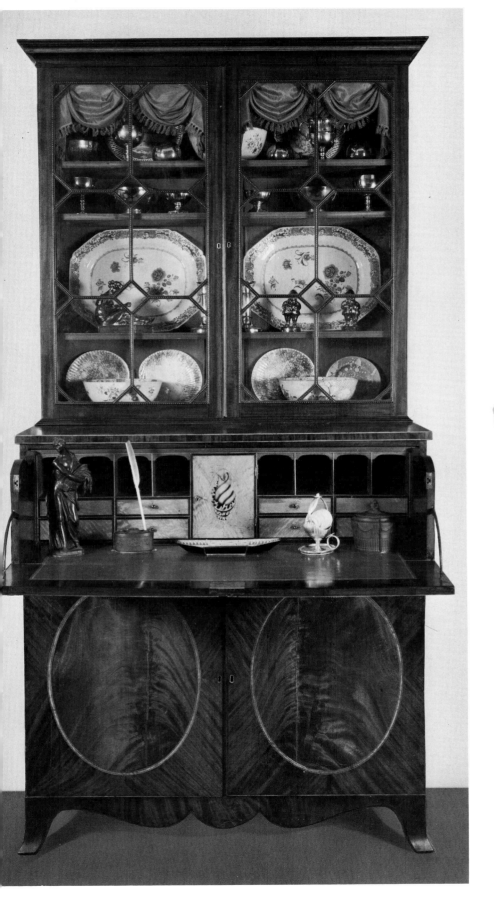

AMERICAN, CA. 1790-1799
Hepplewhite side chair,
from Salem, Massachusetts.
The Metropolitan Museum of Art
Lee Fund, 1937

GEORGE HEPPLEWHITE (?-1786)

Very little is known about the life
and actual work of Hepplewhite.
Here again it is assumed that his book "The
Cabinet-Maker's and Upholsterer's Guide",
published by his wife, who took over the
management of the workshop after him,
made him famous. Some of his designs
closely resemble those of Robert Adam
(or vice-versa). In any case, his
designs were of a very high quality,
fine proportions, and very popular.

ENGLISH, 1775
Armchair made of solid rosewood
and veneered with rosewood.
The inlaywork is satinwood
and probably boxwood.
The architectural ornament
inlayed into the apron
is the Vitruvian Scroll, designed
by Vitruvius Pollio who was
Julius Caesar's architect.
Courtesy Victoria and Albert Museum

THOMAS SHERATON (1751-1806)

Thomas Sheraton was born at Stocton-on-Tees.
He went to London about 1790, and made a
name for himself as an excellent
cabinetmaker, designer and draughtsman.
He gave up cabinetmaking, however,
in favor of designing furniture.
He published his "Cabinet-Maker and
Upholsterer's Drawing Book" in four parts,
the first volume appearing in 1791.
Sheraton's inventiveness and elegant designs
made his book an instant success.

AMERICAN, CA. 1795-1800
Sheraton mahogany arm chair,
made in New York City
*The Metropolitan Museum of Art
Gift of the Members of the Committee of the
Bertha King Benkard Memorial Fund, 1946*

AMERICAN, CA. 1790-1800
Sheraton sofa. Mahogany with satinwood inlay.
From Newburyport, Massachusetts.
The Metropolitan Museum of Art   Gift of Mrs. Russell Sage, 1909

ENGLISH, CA. 1660
Walnut chair twisted (spirally turned)
with cane back and seat.
Courtesy Victoria and Albert Museum

ENGLISH, CA. 1725
Walnut chair, carved
and beautifully veneered
with walnut burl.
Courtesy Victoria and Albert Museum

ENGLISH, CA. 1750
President's chair, of mahogany,
with carved and gilded details.
Made for the president of Lyons Inn,
a London legal society.
Courtesy Victoria and Albert Museum

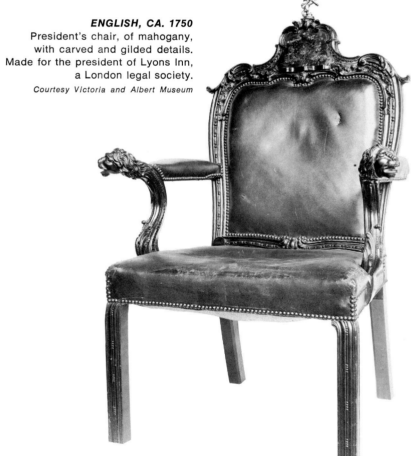

The Firm of WILLIAM VILE and JOHN COBB

Vile and Cobb worked as partners from about
1750 to 1778. They were very successful,
producing furniture of very high quality,
good proportions, with an excellent finish.

ENGLISH, XVIII CENTURY

This beautiful breakfront brings to mind what must have been the beginnings of this type of design.
When the ancient woodworker discovered that a post or column could support as much roof as a solid wall,
he may have tied together cane or bamboo, creating a naturally fluted column;
perhaps he left a few leaves on top. From these early natural posts evolved
the great variety of columns which have been popular with artisans through the ages.
But these columns have been refined to serve a purely decorative purpose
on this imposing architectural breakfront made of mahogany, another
example of the masterly skill of the partners in the firm of Vile and Cobb.
The fluted columns have wheat husks on the lower part of the fluting and acanthus
leaves in the Corinthian capitals. With Rococo carvings, it is an impressive
and distinguished piece among the treasures of English cabinetmaking.

In Windsor Castle
Crown Copyright Reserved

ENGLISH, CA. 1770-1775
This very beautiful mahogany Bombé commode made by John Cobb has a high place among the masterpieces of English cabinetmaking. It appears on the cover of the book, "Georgian Cabinet-Makers" by Ralph Edwards and Margaret Jourdain.
Courtesy Victoria and Albert Museum

Top detail, showing the exquisite veneer work of John Cobb.

ENGLISH, CA. 1760
This ponderous looking mahogany library table was made by William Vile.
It is noteworthy that the Baroque style carvings, Roman arches,
and Grecian key carved into the frieze blend so well together.
Metropolitan Museum of Art   Rogers Fund, 1924

Enlarged views of carving detail.

ENGLISH, CA. 1743
Hanging cabinet of architectural form surmounted with the figures of three great architects: Palladio, Fiammingo and Inigo Jones, carved in ivory by J. C. Verskovis. Veneered with kingwood veneer; carved ivory medallions and plaques are inserted into the front. Made for Horace Walpole by an unidentified craftsman of great ability.
Courtesy Victoria and Albert Museum

ENGLISH, CA. 1775
Design proposal for this cabinet
by John Linnell.
Courtesy Victoria and Albert Museum

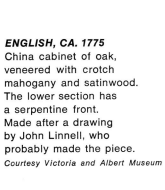

ENGLISH, CA. 1775
China cabinet of oak,
veneered with crotch
mahogany and satinwood.
The lower section has
a serpentine front.
Made after a drawing
by John Linnell, who
probably made the piece.
Courtesy Victoria and Albert Museum

ENGLISH, CA. 1770
Commode made of pine with inserted panels of Chinese lacquer and gold on a black ground.
Courtesy Victoria and Albert Museum

ENGLISH, CA. 1653
Chest of drawers, made of oak in Dutch style,
inlaid with chestnut, ebony,
mother-of-pearl and engraved bone.
The date 1653 is engraved in the center of the
right-hand frieze drawer, as shown
in the enlarged view at lower right.
Courtesy Victoria and Albert Museum

ENGLISH, CA. 1660-1680
Chest of drawers, made of oak
veneered with ebony and palisander,
with molding of fruitwood.
It is in Dutch or late Jacobean style.
Courtesy Victoria and Albert Museum

ENGLISH, LATE XVII CENTURY
Writing cabinet and chest,
veneered with walnut and mulberry,
and decorated with floral
and arabesque or seaweed marquetry. It has bun feet.
Courtesy Victoria and Albert Museum

ENGLISH, CA. 1675
Writing cabinet (scriptor) on stand.
Made for Ham House.
Courtesy Victoria and Albert Museum

The cabinet is veneered with
"oyster" pieces of kingwood veneer.
This is achieved by slicing a
small branch of the tree diagonally,
like salami, and then
fitting the pieces together.

ENGLISH, CA. 1679

Sleeping chairs, carved and gilded, with adjustable backs that fold down to form a bed. They were made for the Duke of Lauderdale. At Ham House, Petershan.

Courtesy Victoria and Albert Museum

ENGLISH, CA. 1680
Arm chair made of walnut
and covered in black leather.
It has iron ratchets for adjusting
the back for sleeping or reclining.
Courtesy Victoria and Albert Museum

ENGLISH, CA. 1650
Carved arm chair in the High Renaissance style.
Originally it was gilded. Designed by Francis Cleyn.
Courtesy Victoria and Albert Museum

ENGLISH, CA. 1650-1660
Chair-table? The back of this chair tilts
forward onto the arms to create a table.
(You eat standing?) Made of oak with applied
split prism, pyramid and other decoration.
Courtesy Victoria and Albert Museum

ENGLISH, CA. 1775
Arm chair of mahogany in the Hepplewhite style.
The motif of the Prince of Wales,
three ostrich feathers, is carved into the back.
Courtesy Victoria and Albert Museum

ENGLISH, CA. 1775
Arm chair of mahogany,
somewhat on the Louis XV style,
but with beautifully flowing lines.
*The Metropolitan Museum of Art
Collection of Irwin Untermyer*

ENGLISH, CA. 1791-1794
Chair of mahogany in the Sheraton style,
the back carved with the Prince of Wales' feathers.
Courtesy Victoria and Albert Museum

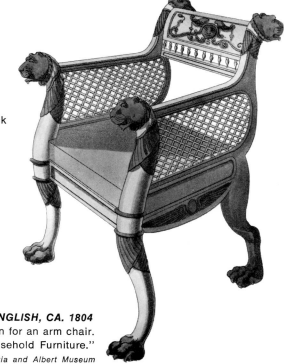

ENGLISH, CA. 1806
Arm chair, carved, painted black
and gilded in "Egyptian" style.
Made for Frome Abbey,
based on Smith's design.
Courtesy Victoria and Albert Museum

ENGLISH, CA. 1804
Design for an arm chair.
From George Smith's "Household Furniture."
Courtesy Victoria and Albert Museum

ENGLISH, CA. 1777
Arm chair design by Robert Adam for the
State Bedroom at Osterley, dated 24th April 1777.
The drawing is in the Soane Museum.
Courtesy Victoria and Albert Museum

ENGLISH, CA. 1777
Arm chair, made according to the design
of Robert Adam, showing very minor
changes from the original concept.
Courtesy Victoria and Albert Museum

ENGLISH, CA. 1810
Globe-shaped mahogany work table.
Made for Queen Charlotte, who ordered it as a birthday
present for the Princess Augusta in 1810.
One of the most difficult operations in woodworking
is the shaping of a globe by hand: it requires
perfect control of hands and tools.
Orange slice shaped pieces of mahogany were fitted
and glued together to form the globe.
It has a band of ebony inlaid in which the signs
of the zodiac engraved on ivory disks are set.
A masterpiece of skill. In Windsor Castle.
Crown Copyright Reserved

A detail showing the delicate
carving of this dumb-waiter.

ENGLISH, CA. 1740
All mahogany dumb-waiter.
Vase shaped shafts,
carved with acanthus leaves.
The finely carved dragon's feet
are unusual in that they hold
square blocks instead
of the customary balls.
*The Metropolitan Museum of Art
Collection of Irwin Untermyer*

ENGLISH, CA. 1700
Walnut cabinet veneered with
inlaywork of ivory, mother-of-pearl,
sycamore, ash, and other woods.
It was made for the marriage of Margaret Trotter and George Lawson, and their mirror initials are
worked into the doors. Very fine workmanship is displayed throughout this cabinet, especially by the cross-grain
veneering of the frieze molding. The shelves on the tops of the arched pediments held Chinese porcelain vases:
Courtesy Victoria and Albert Museum

The doors open reveal the same fine quality veneer inlaywork as the outside, twenty-three drawers and a door, each with a different motif.

Noteworthy, the many various kinds of birds represented.

CHRONOLOGY OF TRENDS IN FURNITURE MAKING IN ENGLAND, AND RELATED PERIODS

TUDOR — ELIZABETHAN	1509 — 1603
JACOBEAN	1603 — 1649
COMMONWEALTH	1649 — 1660
CAROLEAN	1660 — 1688
WILLIAM AND MARY	1689 — 1702
QUEEN ANNE	1702 — 1715
GEORGIAN	1715 — 1795

Georgian included:

CHIPPENDALE	1740 — 1779
ADAMS	1760 — 1792
HEPPLEWHITE	1770 — 1786
SHERATON	1780 — 1806

ENGLISH REGENCY	1793 — 1830
VICTORIAN	1830 — 1890

*JACOBEAN is derived from Jacobus, the Latin name of James I;
CAROLEAN, from Carolus, the Latin name of Charles.*

AMERICAN, CA. 1625-1675
Oak cradle of frame and panel construction.
The panels are beveled on the backside to fit the grooves.

*The Metropolitan Museum of Art
Gift of Mrs. Russell Sage, 1909*

AMERICA

The early cabinetmakers of America should command the most respect: uprooted from comparatively advanced countries, the settler had to carve a civilization out of the wilderness, or at least make it livable. First came shelter, usually a log cabin, Carpenter or not, he had to build his own, while he cultivated and planted his fields. Furniture making had to wait for the long winter days and nights when he would have time to make and repair tools. Then came the most essential furniture, usually a cradle for the newest member of the family, and a dough trough for the lady of the house, so that she could bake that delicious bread. A chest for storage was a very essential item, therefore it usually was decorated. There was also a pine settle to sit by the fire, after all work was done, and talk about the good old days? Those were the pioneer days, and everybody was his own cabinetmaker, carpenter and "anything-else-maker" as well. Whatever had to be done was done. This situation lasted in most areas for a couple of hundred years, due to the constant immigration and expansion of the populated territory.

141

AMERICAN, CA. 1780-1800
Dough trough from Dauphin County, Pennsylvania.
Nicely dovetailed and painted in Dutch style.
The Metropolitan Museum of Art Gift of Mrs. Robert W. de Forest, 1933

AMERICAN, LATE XVII CENTURY
Pine settle, purely functional
and completely devoid of all ornamentation.
The Metropolitan Museum of Art Gift of Mrs. Russell Sage, 1909

In the eastern part of the country, where settlements crystallized into organized communities, time and means were found to promote a gentler way of living, the arts and crafts established themselves and another great tradition of cabinetmaking arose. The inventive genius of the American craftsman and, later, of American industry, had its seed in the early pioneers. Freedom has such an influence on people, not bound by old habits and tradition, they are more apt to try out and advance new methods, improve on old tools, and create new ones. *The storage chest,* an important piece as far as the protection of possessions is concerned, was experimented with. First, they put a drawer under it and called it a Mule Chest. Apparently the drawer was not very smooth-running, but obstinate as a mule. Soon they put two drawers under the chest, carved it elaborately, and we have the famous Hadley chests that were made in Hadley, Massachusetts. Eventually, it shed the chest-box on top, and retained the drawers only, standing on legs. It emerged as the typically American Lowboy that grew up to be the typically American Highboy. Also characteristic is the blockfront furniture, usually with shell carving.

AMERICAN, CA. 1700-1750
Saw-buck leg table with built-in drawer.
The top slides to expose the drawer.
Made of walnut and oak. From Pennsylvania.
The Metropolitan Museum of Art
Gift of Mrs. Robert W. de Forest, 1933

AMERICAN, CA. 1650-1700
Carver style side chair,
made of ash and hickory.
From New England.
The Metropolitan Museum of Art
Gift of Mrs. Russell Sage, 1909

There is, of course, beauty in the sometimes
crude but simple and strictly functional
furniture of the Pilgrims, in the Wainscot
chairs, in the more sophisticated Windsor
chairs, just as there is in the American
Chippendale, Hepplewhite, or Sheraton chairs.
These trends aside, American furniture
making has been divided into two
main periods, Colonial and Federal.
Everything made before the American
Revolution is called Colonial, and the
latter denotes the styles popular after
the Federal government was established.
A time of great prosperity followed,
and with that came the Hitchock chair,
the first mass-produced furniture in history.
Then came the furniture industries of
Grand Rapids, Michigan. A great profusion
of furniture started rolling off assembly lines,
which would not be bad at all if it did
not set aside quality in favor of cheapness,
and individuality in favor of uniformity.
Is the price of affluence the deterioration
of quality, among other things, in furniture?

AMERICAN, 1675-1700
Gate-leg table with oval top.
24½″ high, 25″ wide, 33″ long.
The Metropolitan Museum of Art
Gift of Mrs. Russell Sage, 1909

AMERICAN, XVII CENTURY
Walnut wainscot armchairs, from Chester County, Pennsylvania. These are not a pair, and several variations in design are apparent.
Pilgrim chest made of oak and pine, ca. 1650, from Connecticut.
The Metropolitan Museum of Art

AMERICAN LATE XVIII CENTURY
Oak, veneered and inlaid chest of drawers.

*The Metropolitan Museum of Art, Gift of Mrs. J.
Insler Blair, 1948*

AMERICAN, EARLY XIX CENTURY
From the Shaker Community of Mt. Lebanon N.Y. The extremely
plain and functional design of this piece, makes it a classic
of its kind.

The Brooklyn Museum, Gift of Mrs. Oscar Bernstein

AMERICAN, 1700-1750
Chippendale arm chair,
of maple with woven rush seat.
The Metropolitan Museum of Art
Gift of Mrs. Russell Sage, 1909

AMERICAN, 1765-1770
Chippendale style arm chair with pierced and finely carved back.
From Boston, Massachusetts.
The Metropolitan Museum of Art
Fletcher Fund, 1944

Detail showing carving on the chest at left. It may be noted that the design motifs of both top and bottom borders are not perfectly symmetrical, adding to the unsophisticated charm of the piece.

AMERICAN, EARLY XVIII CENTURY
Tall clock, mahogany case.
Made by William Claggett of Newport, Rhode Island.

The Metropolitan Museum of Art
The Sylmaris Collection
Gift of George Coe Graves, 1930

AMERICAN, XVIII CENTURY
Architectural woodwork:
doorway, from Ridgeville, Maryland.

The Metropolitan Museum of Art
Rogers Fund, 1918

147

AMERICAN, XVIII CENTURY
Charles Allen Munn Room, from the American Wing of the Metropolitan Museum of Art.
The woodwork was taken from a house at 237 South Third Street, Philadelphia.
The Metropolitan Museum of Art

AMERICAN, XVIII CENTURY
Colonial furniture from Pennsylvania:

Windsor table, made of whitewood, maple and ash.

Windsor settee, made of whitewood, maple and ash.

Candlestand, made of maple and painted black.

AMERICAN, 1725-1750
Wall panelling from Newington, Connecticut.

AMERICAN, MID XVIII CENTURY
Excellent Mahogany Highboy with a fine example of shell carving.
The Brooklyn Museum, Henry L. Batterman Fund

AMERICAN MID XVIII CENTURY
Mahogany Bureau of extremely fine cabinetwork.
The Brooklyn Museum

AMERICAN, 1750-1775
A very beautiful mahogany block-front desk
of unusually fine workmanship and proportions.
36¼″ high, 32¼″ wide, 18¾″ deep.
The Metropolitan Museum of Art
Kennedy Fund, 1918

AMERICAN, 1750
Tall-case clock of walnut, made by Henry Hill of New York City.
Two Queen Anne style side chairs, painted maple, from Connecticut. Ca. 1725.
The Metropolitan Museum of Art

AMERICAN, 1750-1775
Windsor arm chair, of spruce and oak.
From Pennsylvania.
The Metropolitan Museum of Art
Gift of Mrs. Russell Sage, 1909

AMERICAN, 1770-1780
Mahogany tilt-top table.
The pie-crust top not only
tilts but also revolves.

The Metropolitan Museum of Art
Rogers Fund, 1925

CANADIAN, LATE XVIII CENTURY
Turned arm chair with slat back and rush seat.
Made of birch.

The Metropolitan Museum of Art
The Sylmaris Collection
Gift of George Coe Graves, 1930

AMERICAN, LATE XVIII CENTURY
Tall clock with mahogany case.
Made by Simon Willard (1753-1848)
in Roxbury, Massachusetts.

The Metropolitan Museum of Art
The Sylmaris Collection
Gift of George Coe Graves, 1930

AMERICAN, 1770-1775
Tall clock, walnut.
Made by
John Wood in Philadelphia.

The Metropolitan Museum of Art
Bequest of W. Gedney Beatty, 1941

AMERICAN, XVIII CENTURY
Blockfront chest on chest.
A very good representation of this
style of American furniture, from
the bracket feet to the twisted finials.
The Metropolitan Museum of Art
Rogers Fund, 1919

AMERICAN, XVIII CENTURY
Mahogany tilt-top table
with pie-crust edge.
Probably from Philadelphia.
The Metropolitan Museum of Art
The Sylmaris Collection
Gift of George Coe Graves, 1930

AMERICAN, 1785-1795
Hepplewhite mahogany arm chair.
The Metropolitan Museum of Art
Kennedy Fund, 1918

AMERICAN, XVIII CENTURY
Highboy and lowboy. Very fine examples of American designed and made furniture. Carved walnut and walnut veneered.

AMERICAN, 1795-1800
Mahogany sideboard, inlaid with boxwood (white),
ebony, satinwood, silver and glass panels.
Tambour front knife boxes on top.

The Metropolitan Museum of Art
Gift of Mitchell Taradash and Pulitzer Fund, 1945

AMERICAN, XVIII & XIX CENTURY
Types of hardware used on American furniture.

The Metropolitan Museum of Art

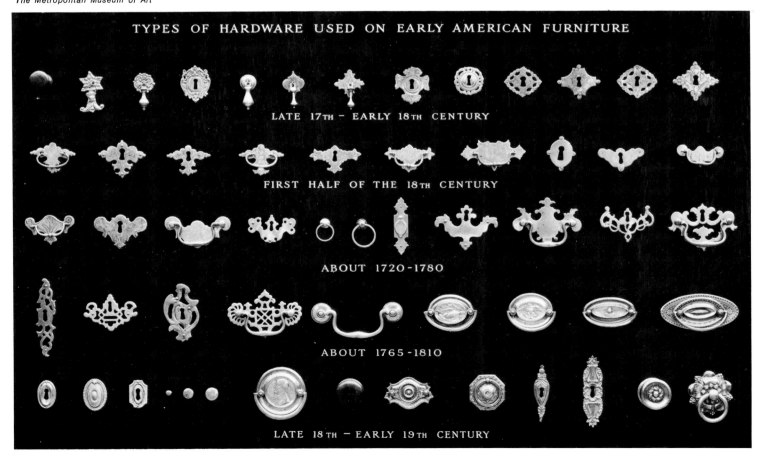

TYPES OF HARDWARE USED ON EARLY AMERICAN FURNITURE

LATE 17TH - EARLY 18TH CENTURY

FIRST HALF OF THE 18TH CENTURY

ABOUT 1720-1780

ABOUT 1765-1810

LATE 18TH - EARLY 19TH CENTURY

SOME OF THE FAMOUS CABINETMAKERS OF AMERICA

JOHN ALDEN (1599-1687)

John Alden, was born in Southampton, England. He came over on the Mayflower in 1620 and was a founder of the Plymouth Colony. Later he lived in Duxbury, Massachusetts, where, besides making furniture, he acted as Assistant Governor of the colony. In 1623, he married Priscilla Mullins after a great romantic and very involved courtship which became a popular legend. Longfellow wrote the poem "The Courtship of Miles Standish" about them. There are a few pieces of furniture in existence attributed to him.

THE ALLIS FAMILY

There was an extensive dynasty of cabinetmakers in the Allis family. The founder was William Allis who came to America on the third voyage of the Mayflower in 1630. He and his two sons, John (1642-1691). and Samuel (1647-1691) and their families moved to Hadley, Massachusetts where they made, among other things to be sure, some of the famed Hadley chests. His grandsons Ichabod (1675-1747) and John (1682-?) continued the family tradition in partnership with Samuel Belding (1657-1737).

GILBERT ASH (1747-1785)

Gilbert Ash was a very successful cabinetmaker who worked in New York City. There are many Chippendale style chairs attributed to him.

JOHN BELTER (1804-1863)

John Belter was born in Würtenberg, Germany, where he served his apprenticeship. Belter came to New York City about 1840; in 1844, he had a workshop on Chatham Square, later two separate shops on Broadway, finally at Third Avenue and 76th Street, where he employed many cabinetmakers and about forty apprentices. He rediscovered the method of laminating many layers of veneer at right angles to each other, clamped in a form, creating curved pieces. His work was complicated and highly ornate in the Baroque and Rococo-Victorian styles.

Belter accomplished an excellent interpretation of Rococo carving by simplification, elimination of minor detail and bold emphasis of design.

AMERICAN, XIX CENTURY
Rosewood Victorian sofa, made by John Belter of New York City.
The Metropolitan Museum of Art   Gift of Mr. and Mrs. Lowell Ross Burch and Miss Jean McLean Morron, 1951

BENJAMIN FROTHINGHAM (1734-1809)

Frothingham's father, also a cabinetmaker, had his workshop in Boston, Massachusetts. Undoubtedly, young Benjamin learned the trade from his father. It is believed that he had his own workshop in Charlestown, Massachusetts by 1756. During the American Revolution, he served in the Colonial army, advancing to the rank of Major. Frothingham was a close friend of George Washington who, in 1784, visited Frothingham at his home and workshop in Charlestown.

THE GODDARDS and TOWNSENDS
(MID 18TH — LATE 19TH CENTURY)

The Goddards and Townsends were two outstanding families of cabinetmakers who lived and worked together at Newport, Rhode Island. Both families were Quakers and were closely related by marriage and friendship. The Goddards are credited with making a great amount of furniture, with the blockfront design. Daniel Goddard, the founder of the family, was a carpenter, but his two sons, three grandsons, and a number of his great grandsons were all fine cabinetmakers. Solomon Townsend was the patriarch of the Townsend family that produced thirteen cabinetmakers in four generations.

LAMBERT HITCHCOCK (1795-1852)

In 1818, Hitchcock established a cabinet and chair factory in Barkhamsted, Connecticut, where, at first, he made chair parts and sold them to other cabinetmakers. He also shipped them to many parts of the country. By 1825, as his factory grew and more and more workers built homes around the factory, a settlement was established which became Hitchcockville. Soon they were making complete chairs, and the first mass produced furniture was born. These chairs were painted and sometimes grained to look like rosewood, or some other woods. Stencilled-on decorations of fruits and flowers were typical. They also made Boston rockers with the same stencilled-on designs.

AMERICAN, XVIII CENTURY
Blockfront secretary of mahogany, attributed to Benjamin Frothingham.
Nelson Gallery, Atkins Museum (Nelson Fund) Kansas City, Missouri

AMERICAN, XVIII CENTURY
Mahogany card table inlaid with satinwood,
bearing the label of Stephen and Thomas Goddard,
the grandsons of the founder of the dynasty
of cabinetmakers, Daniel Goddard.
The Metropolitan Museum of Art   Rogers Fund, 1929

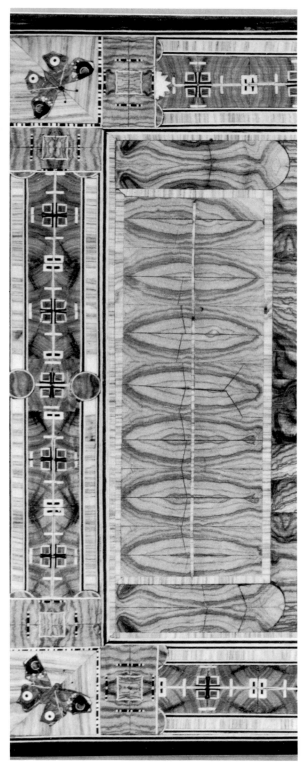

AMERICAN, 1924
Exquisite marquetry table of tulipwood,
violet wood, holly and ebony,
with gold plated brass mounts.
Detail of tabletop shows fine inlaywork.
Made by Clark Jones of New York City.
The Metropolitan Museum of Art
Edward C. Moore, Jr. Gift Fund, 1925

AMERICAN, 1796
Chest on chest from Salem, Massachusetts
This has been described as one of the finest examples of American cabinetmaking and design. Made by William Lemon.
It is noteworthy for the unusually fine crotch-mahogany veneering and excellent workmanship.
The design and carving are attributed to Samuel McIntire.
Courtesy of The Museum of Fine Arts, Boston   The M and M Karolik Collection

SAMUEL McINTIRE (1757-1811)

McIntire was the American counterpart of Robert Adam, the English architect and designer. He outdid Adam, however, in that he not only designed, but also built some twenty mansions on Chestnut Street in Salem, Massachusetts. He designed the interiors and built the furniture for them. He was also a fine woodcarver and designed and carved for other cabinetmakers. His son, Samuel Field McIntire (1780-1819) carried on in his father's workshop and business. Probably some of the pieces attributed to his father were made by him.

AMERICAN, 1800-1820
Side chair made by Duncan Phyfe.
All details indicate his style and workmanship;
the acanthus leaves carved into the solid wood legs,
the reeding and the horns of plenty.
Courtesy of the Brooklyn Museum

DUNCAN PHYFE (1768-1854)

Duncan Phyfe was the most famous American cabinetmaker. He and his family came from Scotland in 1783. They settled in Albany, New York, where his father established a woodworking shop. Duncan probably served part of his apprenticeship there since he had already worked for his father in Scotland. In 1792, he had his own workshop at 2 Broad Street, New York City. From there he moved to Fulton Street where, as he became prosperous, he bought three buildings. The rich and famous clamored for his work. His furniture was always of a high quality with good proportions. He imported mahogany from Santo Domingo and Cuba at great expense, sometimes paying as much as a thousand dollars for a single log. He personally supervised cutting veneer, to take advantage of the grain of the wood in the best possible way. Phyfe worked in many of the prevailing styles, but he never contrasted color veneers, even the banding and crossbanding was done with the same mahogany as the rest of the surface. Another distinctive and easily recognizable feature is the Acanthus Leaf carving on the legs of chairs and tables, which is not raised above the legs, but rather gouged out of the solid wood. Reeding is found on practically all of his furniture. Duncan Phyfe's name is synonymous with fine furniture of the first half of the 19th century.

The chair back with horn of plenty motif favored by Phyfe.

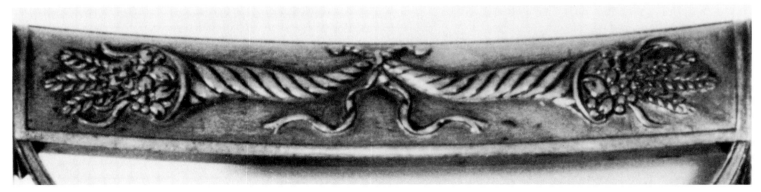

AMERICAN, CA. 1800

Sideboard displaying a combination of good design, fine veneering and carving, plus superb workmanship. This piece, with tambour doors which were an innovation, testifies to the fact that John Seymour was highly deserving of the title, "the finest cabinetmaker in Boston," after the Revolution.

Courtesy of the Museum of Fine Arts, Boston
The M. and M. Karolik Collection

BENJAMIN RANDOLPH

Benjamin Randolph was born in Monmouth County, New Jersey. He established his workshop, called the Golden Eagle, in Philadelphia about 1760-1761. There he made high quality, elaborate, carved Baroque-Rococo Chippendale style furniture. Thomas Jefferson commissioned Randolph to make several pieces of furniture. The table upon which the Declaration of Independence was signed, was made by Benjamin Randolph.

JOHN and THOMAS SEYMOUR —

John Seymour and his son, Thomas, worked as partners from about 1800 on. John was considered the greatest designer and cabinetmaker in Boston, after the American Revolution. One of the characteristics of his work is the robin's egg blue paint used on the interiors of some of his furniture. Other features are inlaid pilasters, reeded tambour doors, delicate proportions, and exceptionally fine workmanship.

TOOLS WERE NOT
MADE FOR FOOLS
WHO CANNOT ABIDE
BY SAFETY RULES

LK

CRAFTSMANSHIP

We have seen in the foregoing chapters
the quality of handwork which can be
created with hand tools. Now let us explore
the method and manner of making such fine,
useful, and even artistic pieces of furniture.
It may sound preposterous in this day and age,
when so much machinery is readily available,
to try to advance the idea of working with
hand tools. But the discarding of machinery
is not advocated, and neither is turning back
the clock of progress (however nice that
would be). The real intent here is to point
out the much neglected difference between
machinemade and handmade articles.
What is the importance of handwork in an age
when automation is pushing personal talent
and skill into obscurity, where the ultimate
goal seems to be a button-pushing finger
to create the things called civilization?
In such an age, craftsmanship, important
either as a rewarding hobby or a trade for a
lifetime, a means by which one can express
his creative ability and thereby make his
(and everybody's) world a nicer place
to live in, is of uppermost significance.

TOOLS

The old adage "practice makes perfect"
was never truer than in the case
of working with tools. One cannot
read and know instantly where physical
movements and discipline are involved.
There may be perfect understanding
through reading about tools, their purpose
and function, but only through exercise
can one acquire proficiency in their use.
Tools have to become the extension of our
hands. They eventually hook up to our
nervous system and perform at the command
of our minds. The ultimate aim is to be like
the old time craftsman who made his own
tools to suit himself, by weight, shape,
and so on, and worked with them for years
like a virtuoso with a musical instrument.
Today, however, there are ready made tools
available, some fine ones to be sure, and
one should buy only the best to be found.
Working with a set of good tools can be
a profitable and pleasurable experience.

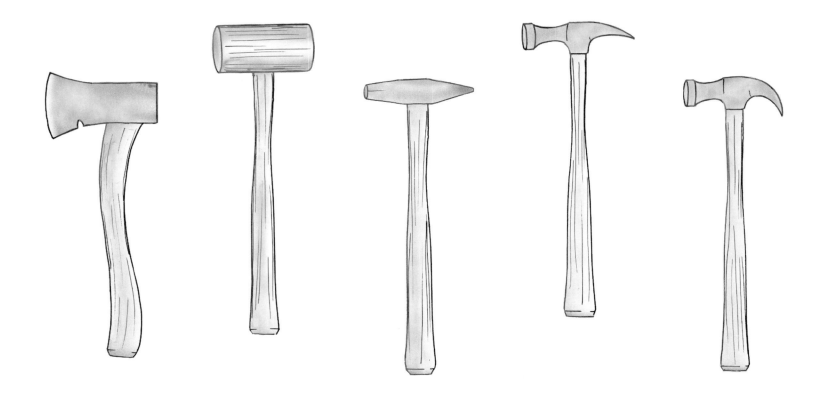

THE HAMMER

The hammer is the oldest tool used by mankind. After so many thousands of years, working with a hammer comes to us naturally. Put a hammer into the hands of a two year old boy, and he will immediately bang away with it, happily and contentedly. The idea of hammering is the same today as it was in the times of cavemen. The tool itself, however, has been vastly improved. There are a great variety of hammer styles available today, for many jobs and many trades. For all practical purposes, we should consider the two most generally useful ones in woodworking, the *straight claw* and the *curved claw*. The one with the straight claw can be used for splitting wood, pulling nails, etc. Also the straight claw makes it easier to do heavy work because the hammer travels in an arc. There is more weight on the outside of the arc, and that increases the speed and thereby the weight and hitting power. This, of course, is not always desirable. The curved claw hammer is a shade

slower, but it is easier to pull nails with. The face of this hammer is slightly convex. You can drive a nail flush with the surface of the wood without leaving any hammer marks, regardless of the fact that sometimes the hammer does not meet the wood exactly perpendicular. The hammer, especially the face of it, *must — must — must* be clean of all dirt, paint, or glue, and completely free of chips and scratches. Otherwise, it can be a dangerous tool, to which many a sore thumb and bad work will testify. The handle, if it is wood, should be ash, maple, or hickory, which is best. When a new handle is to be set into the hammerhead, the handle should have saw cuts for wedges, preferably two, either parallel or in X form. After the handle is tapped lightly into the head, lift it up so that the hammerhead hangs down freely and give short stiff blows to the end of the handle with a wooden mallet. The head will climb up on the handle; when it cuts into the handle and a little woodshaving curls up, it is ready

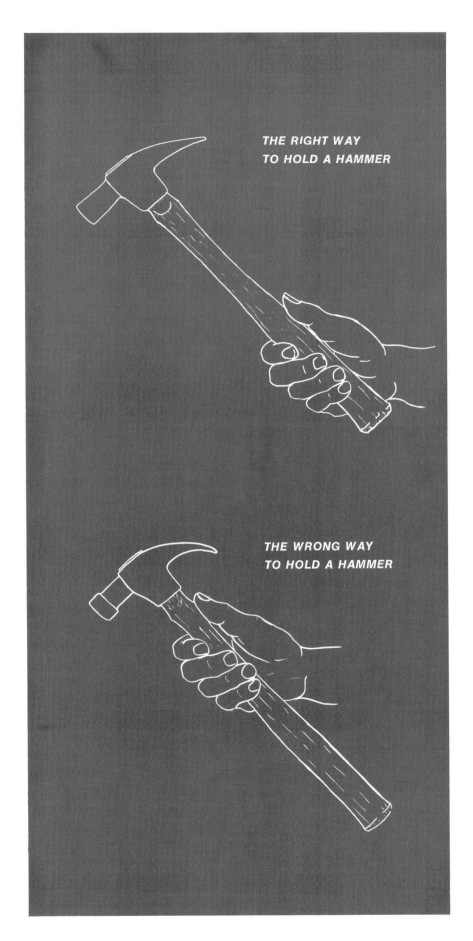

THE RIGHT WAY TO HOLD A HAMMER

THE WRONG WAY TO HOLD A HAMMER

for you to drive in the wedges, and to trim off the wood protruding from the head. You may now shape the handle with a fine rasp file, to suit your taste and fit your hand. Sandpaper it well, soak it in a light oil, and you have a hammer you will enjoy using. If you choose a hammer with a handle made of metal or some other material, try before you buy, for shape and weight. Give it a few practice swings. It should feel completely comfortable, not too light and not too heavy. In general, it should be between 13 and 16 ounces. Working with a hammer may come naturally, but good habits have to be acquired. The hammer should be held at the end of the handle. When nailing, the nail should be held with the first three fiingers of the left hand (provided you are right handed). Give a couple of light taps, and when the nail is about one-third in, let go and drive it in with slightly heavier blows. The nail should feel hard through the hammer and give in by going into the wood. If the feel is soft and spongy, the nail will bend and should be pulled out. It is best to pull a nail with a block of wood under the hammerhead, so that it does not mar the work surface. Especially in the beginning, some attention should be given to the motion of hammering. The hammer should be lifted up to a height required for a sufficient amount of force to drive in the nails. That can only come through practice. It can be anywhere from three to four inches to all the way up where the arm and hammer are raised above and behind the head. The shoulder, the arm, and wrist have to work in unison *always* parallel with the body or close to it. First the arm at the shoulder describes the circular motion, followed by the elbow, and finally the wrist creates a whip-like action that gives speed to the downward flight of the hammerhead. Finally, the hammer should land on the nail or work surface with the handle and the face parallel to it. One should be able to hammer in all directions, for example, all 360° of a vertical circle. Skill is shown by using the least number of blows to drive in a nail.

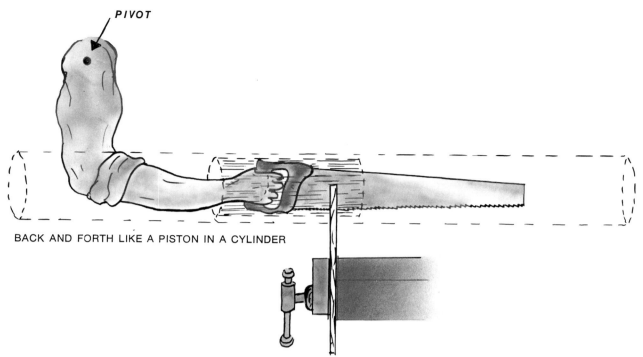

PIVOT

BACK AND FORTH LIKE A PISTON IN A CYLINDER

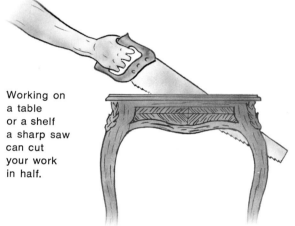

Working on
a table
or a shelf
a sharp saw
can cut
your work
in half.

THE SAW

Of first and foremost importance, as with all tools, is the discipline of body movements, especially with the handsaw. While sawing, one should exert the least power for the most work. To do this economically, the movements of the arm have to be controlled consciously, in the beginning at least. It is very, very important that the arm and elbow go back and forth parallel to the body, *never* to and fro sideways. The forearm and the wrist have to work like a valve in a piston, straight back and forth. Years ago, when an apprentice could not get the idea, they would put a raspfile under his arm and he had to keep it there while sawing. The body should be as motionless as possible while the arm works. The saw must be held firmly and cut on the forward push only. It has to be pulled back very lightly without decreasing the speed, with only its own weight resting on the work.

When working with a two-man saw, each man cuts when pulling and eases up when the other pulls, without letting go of his handle.

For general woodworking, there are two kinds of handsaws: the *ripsaw,* for cutting with the length of the wood, with the grain, and the *crosscut saw,* as its name implies, to cut across the grain.

The difference is in the filing.

We have to imagine a saw as many little chisels set one behind the other. For ripping, the teeth are filed at a right angle to the blade; thus the teeth meet and cut the wood straight on. Obviously, this would not do for crosscutting. The teeth would tear the woodgrain on the underside of the work. Therefore the little chisels are set at an angle most suitable to cut the woodgrain on the outside of the kerf (saw cut).

In all cases the teeth have to be set (bent sideways) alternating to both sides, so that the kerf is wider than the sawblade is thick, so it will not bind. There are a great variety of saws for many purposes, such as coping saw, keyhole saw, back saw, and their use is usually self-explanatory.

Good working habits with clean and sharp saws will give much satisfaction while working.

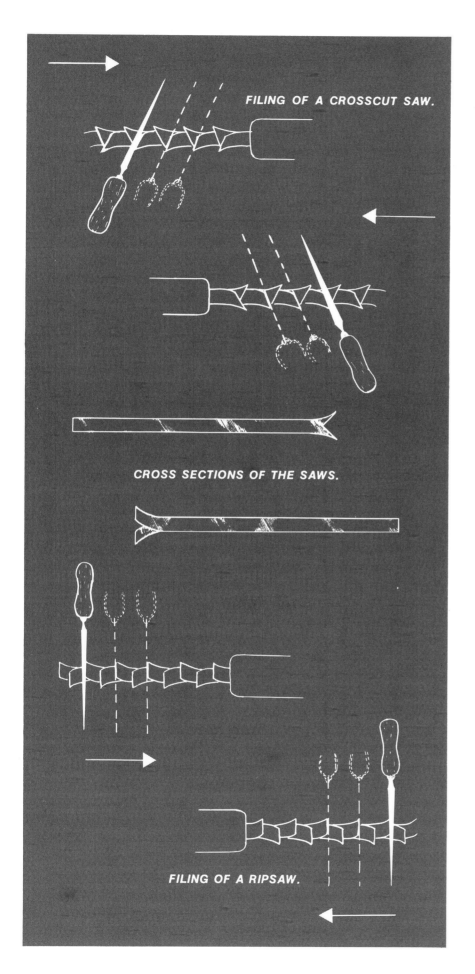

FILING OF A CROSSCUT SAW.

CROSS SECTIONS OF THE SAWS.

FILING OF A RIPSAW.

FILING A SAW

Filing a saw is really a simple matter. However, it does require a certain amount of self-controlled movements, though these are easily mastered. The saw should be tightened in a saw clamp, the end first and the handle to your right. It is almost always advisable to joint the teeth: remove the handle from the file, lay it on the teeth lengthwise, push it the whole length of the saw once or twice, always starting from the saw handle. This will make the teeth even. Replace the handle on the file. The gullet (the space between the teeth) should not be more than one-eighth of an inch above the clamp, and level with your elbow. Place the end of the file in front of the first tooth that is set toward you, if this is a ripsaw. Hold the file at right angles to the saw — it should lay in there completely touching all sides — push forward the complete length of the file once or twice, but no more if possible. Skip the next gullet and file the one after it, always the ones set toward you. When you reach the handle, turn the saw around in the clamp, again starting from the end and going toward the handle on your left, filing the teeth set toward you and skipping the others. Filing the crosscut saw, you may follow the same procedure, but instead of filing at a right angle you hold the file at approximately 45° to the blade, facing halfway toward the handle. The whole secret of filing lies in some simple rules. Obviously, the file must travel level and not wobble at all. But more important, as you file the first tooth, the same amount of back and forth motion and the power exerted must be maintained throughout the filing. Any little deviation from this will cause uneven teeth which will make a ragged cut. The little effort required in learning these disciplined motions is amply rewarded by the pleasure of working with a good sharp saw. Anybody who ever had to cut with a dull one can appreciate the difference.

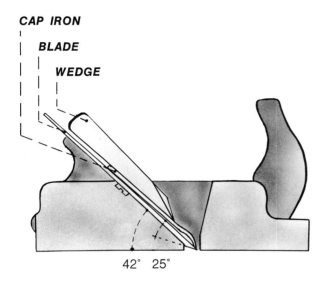

Cross section of a modern wooden plane, showing the correct assembly

CAP IRON

BLADE

WEDGE

42° 25°

THE PLANE

The plane, of all tools, achieved the most sophistication. It had its humble beginnings as a simple block of wood (although at times decorated with great pride) notched out for a blade that was held in place by a wedge at a certain angle, the sharp edge of the blade protruding on the bottom with just enough space in front of it for the shaving to go through. This developed into today's metal plane, which is completely adjustable with screws, nuts, and levers. But the metal plane itself is standardized: there is only one shape, weight and form for everybody. By contrast, with the wooden plane, one can appreciate the difference of feeling wood in the hands instead of cold metal. The other advantages of the wooden plane lie in the fact that it can be individualized and adjusted to one's own taste. Its shape can be made to conform to the hands and grip,

its weight can be increased by soaking it in oil. A good, well balanced, well adjusted and sharp wooden plane will make a long, fine shaving, and leave a smooth silk-like surface behind. This is perfection in a plane, which with a little practice can very easily be mastered.

There are two kinds of wooden planes: the *simple* or *scrub* plane has a single blade which may be sharpened to a slightly convex cutting edge. It has a somewhat larger throat and is used to remove a lot of stock but it does not leave a smooth surface. The *smooth* or *double* plane is so called because it has a double blade; that is, a cap iron is fastened to the blade only about a hairline from the cutting edge and does not allow the blade to cut a heavier shaving. The fact here is that the finer the shaving, the smoother the surface will be.

The blade in a wooden plane is adjusted with a hammer: by tapping the back of the plane, the blade and wedge will ride up and loosen; by tapping the wedge down, the blade is tightened; and it may be tapped lightly to the desired protrusion, and sideways so that the edge is perfectly parallel with the bottom of the plane. How much the blade should protrude can be judged by eye first, and then by practice. Turn the plane upside down, raise it so that the front of the plane is facing your nose and the back of it sloping downward. You should see the blade as a fine hairline. If it is more, tap on the back of the plane; if it is less, tap on the blade. The best guide is to try it out on a piece of wood. Oddly enough, the simpler the tool, the more practice, knowledge and skill are required in handling it.

Therefore, a complicated looking metal plane is actually a simplification of the above. One of the joys of woodworking is being able to use a good sharp plane on a nice piece of wood. When planing a surface, the wood has to be clamped firmly in the workbench. Start planing from the nearest edge and, if possible, from end to end. Place the plane on the starting line completely sitting on

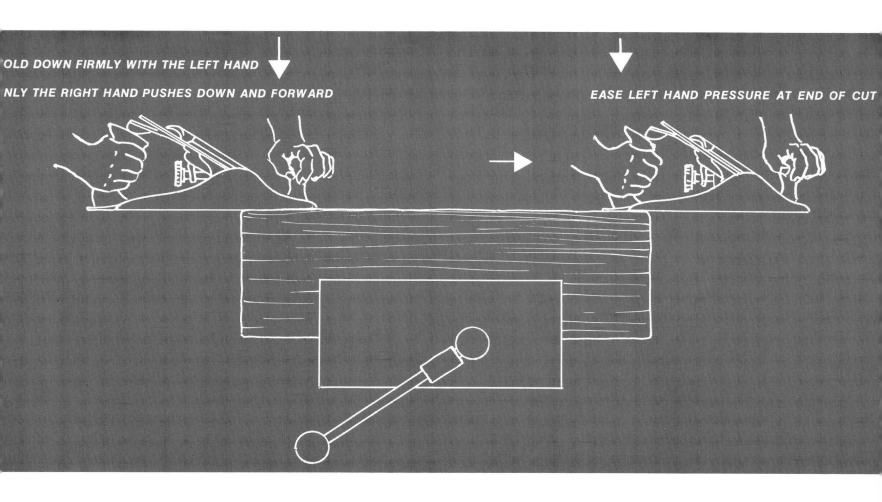

the wood; holding it firmly, tilt it very slightly away from you so that the plane rests on the edge furthest from you. Now pull it back until the blade clears the wood without touching it. Then let the tip of the plane sit on the wood. Hold it down firmly with the left hand and with the right give it a strong fast push forward. While the plane travels, both hands push down on it and forward with the same effort, but when it nears the end of the work the left hand has to ease up on it and only the right hand pushes down and forward until the blade clears the wood. This is done in order not to tip the plane down after it passes the wood. Now bring the plane back, only its own weight resting on the outside edge, so that the blade does not touch the wood on its backward travel. Do it the same way as on the first push, but next to it and so on. All this, the push forward and bringing back the plane, should take less than one second on a piece of wood about three feet long. Planing an edge has to be done with a long jointer plane. It will make a straighter edge than a short smoothing plane. On pulling back the jointer plane, raise the back of it just enough so the blade does not touch, or you will have to sharpen the blade very often. Planing the end grain of the wood has to be done from both ends, so as not to chip or splinter the wood on the far side. A short piece of wood should always be planed as if it had a convex shape; in other words, the emphasis must be on the center of the work, and in that way it is sure to end up straight. Edges have to be tested with the square and flat surfaces with a straight-edge. There are many types of planes for a variety of special purposes, from adjustable rabbet planes to adjustable grooving planes, and many kinds of molding planes. Although it is not really a plane, but a draw knife in a housing, we may also include here the spoke shave, an excellent tool for shaping and smoothing irregular and curved pieces. Good sharp planes are always fun to work with.

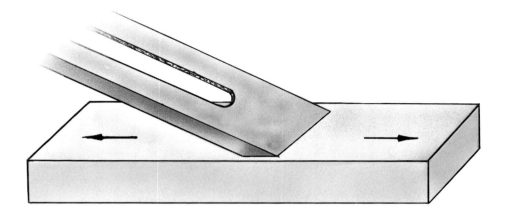

SHARPENING

Actually, one should not even attempt woodworking or any other hobby or trade where sharp tools are used before mastering the art of sharpening and maintaining tools. Otherwise, it would be like facing a delicious steak with a dull knife. Half the fun in woodworking lies in using good, keen tools.

For sharpening a plane blade, an oilstone and light oil are needed. The best lubricant is a light motor oil mixed with kerosene. Have the stone securely fastened and soaked with oil on the rough side, and set the bevel of the blade on the stone. The blade's position should be about 25° to 30° to the stone, and a little at an angle toward the length of the stone. In this position, held firmly, the blade is pushed back and forth without *any* rocking motion (a rocking motion would give a rounded bevel) until a wire edge is raised on the flat side that can be felt by placing the thumb on the blade and pulling it toward the edge.

Now reverse the blade, lay it flat on the stone, taking several strokes while holding the blade down firmly. Check to see that the wire is gone (some may have gone over to the bevel side), and then turn the blade back to the bevel side, giving a few light strokes, always being aware of not rocking the blade the slightest. This turning of the blade must be a fast and precise motion, for the blade has to find its exact position each time. Turn the stone over with the smooth side up, give a few light strokes first on the bevel side, then on the flat side of the blade, alternating until all wire or burr is gone. This may be tested again by pulling the thumb toward and away from the cutting edge, *never against it.* All chisels and tools can be sharpened in this manner, and if the skill is mastered and it is done properly, you should be able to shave the hair from the top of your wrist with the edge of a well sharpened blade.

THE CHISEL

Some of the main uses for the chisel are in making wood joints, since practically all joints, such as dovetail, mortise, half lap, and so on, require the use of the chisel. Of course, there are a million and one other uses for it, from setting hinges, mortising locks, and cutting, to carving. Gouges for carving are also chisels, bent to various shapes.
The ways of holding a chisel are as varied as its use, the basic and most obvious one being to grasp it firmly by the handle with the left hand and hitting, or better, tapping it with a mallet held in the right hand.

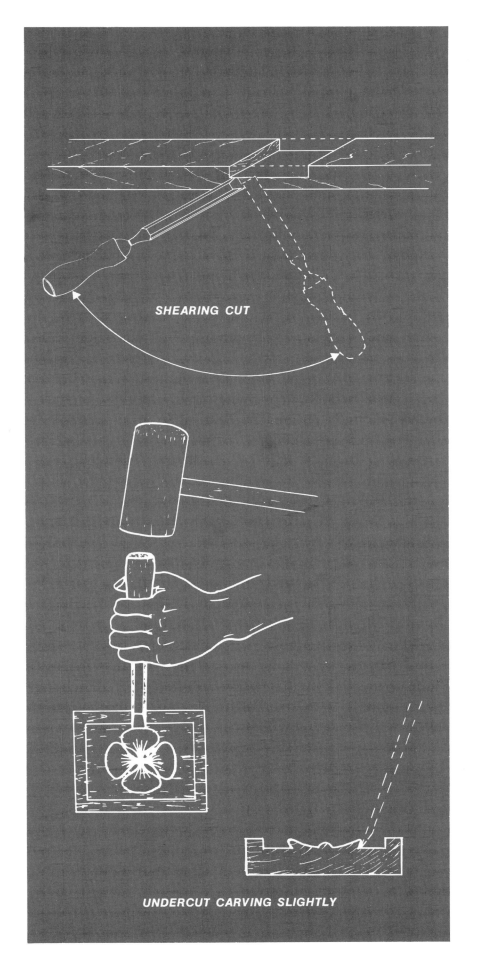

SHEARING CUT

UNDERCUT CARVING SLIGHTLY

This is so in mortising and other deep cutting, and also for precision cutting, such as notching for hinges or other hardware. In setting hinges the size of the hinge must be marked exactly, the width and thickness with a marking gauge and the length with a pencil. The chisel should be held perfectly vertical and cut with light taps all around, but a hairbreadth inside (on the waste side) of the markings, the flat side of the chisel always toward the outside facing the pencil marks. Always leave the pencil mark — never cut it away. This rule also applies to carving. In carving, if it is not a very deep cut, the chisel can be held with both hands. Usually the left hand holds the lower part of the handle and part of the blade and does most of the guiding. The right hand holds the upper part of the handle and supplies the power. When removing stock, as for example in making a half-lap joint, a very helpful method is the shearing cut. The chisel is held horizontally with the flat side down and at an angle to the work; push the leading corner of the chisel into the wood. Then, using that corner as a pivot, make a part of a circle with the handle. This will give a clean cut even somewhat against the grain and on hard woods. With a little experimentation in these basic methods, greater variety in the usage of chisels will be discovered. Never work with the chisel in one hand, and the other hand holding the work in front of it. If the work must be held with one hand, it should be held behind the direction of the chisel. Never hold the chisel with both hands and pull it toward yourself. There are as many safety rules as there are ways of holding a chisel, but rules are no substitutes for constant awareness and safe habits, the importance of which cannot be emphasized strongly enough. But after the technique of working with chisels and gouges is mastered, great things can be created, and many pleasurable hours spent working with them.

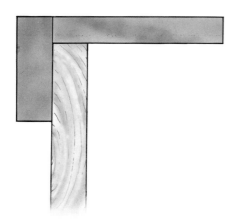

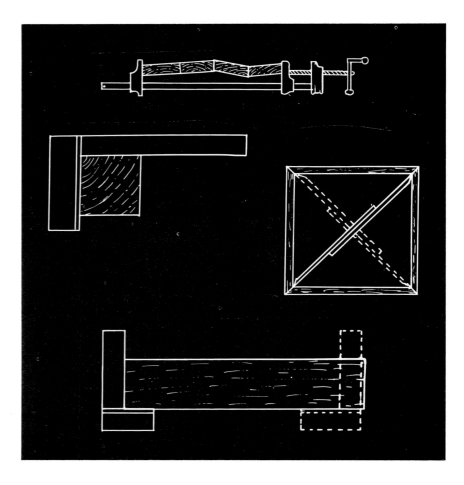

THE SQUARE

The importance of the square becomes obvious as soon as one starts doing any woodworking. The first step in making anything is to prepare the lumber: all edges have to be made straight, square and parallel, and all ends when cut to size, must be perfectly square (unless, of course, the design requires otherwise). To check that an edge is straight, raise one end of the wood to eye level, and by sighting along the whole length of the edge, all bumps and hollows will be quite visible. Irregularities can be best corrected with a long jointer plane. If the edge is convex (a hump in the middle), push the plane from the nearest end to about three-quarters of the way, then start one-third the length from the starting end. This done as many times as needed is the best method to correct a convex edge. However, if the edge is concave (has a hollow), plane each end first and then the whole length.

Now is the time to check for squareness. The shorter and heavier side of the square is called the tongue, the longer and thinner is the body. The tongue is held against the face of the wood and the body resting on the edge. There should be no light coming through between the square and the edge. How vital this is becomes apparent when boards are glued together edge to edge. The next time the square plays an important role is when glueing together a frame or a cabinet. However, if the cabinet is more than twice the size of the square, it is preferable to measure for squareness with a ruler or a strip, checking from opposite corners diagonally.

THE SCRAPER

The scraper, one of the simplest of all tools, rivals the best of them in value in woodworking. The hand scraper is a piece of thin steel usually about one-sixteenth of an inch thick, two and a half inches wide, and six inches long. What did we say before about the simpler a tool, the more there is to working with it? Well, here you have a "lulu." As a matter of fact, when one has mastered the use of a scraper, he may consider himself an accomplished craftsman. All veneer work requires the use of a scraper to clean off glue, take out scratches, and in general make the work smooth before sandpapering. All hardwoods, after planing, should be scraped to remove plane marks, to take out tears where the plane went against the grain of the wood, and so on. The wire or burr that has to be avoided like the dickens on the edge of all cutting tools is the working edge of the scraper. The hand scraper has to be sharpened by standing it on its edge on the rough side of the oilstone, a little at an angle to the

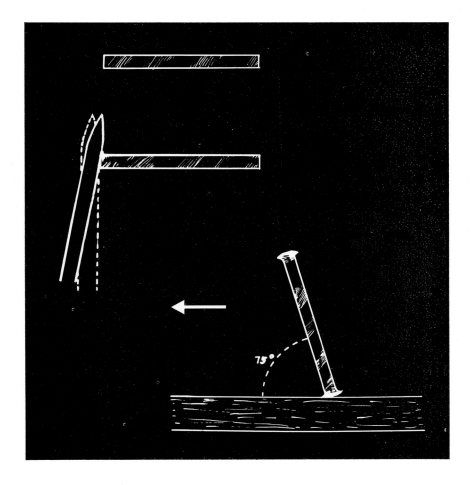

Handscraping can be done two ways,
by pushing or pulling. Either way, the scraper
should make a shaving similar to a plane,
but much finer. When pushing the scraper,
it must be held at about 75° to the wood, but
this is done only when a lot of wood has to
be removed, as in the case of a deep scratch,
because it may leave deep gouges.
However, after a deep scratch is removed,
the surface around it should be evened out
with the pulling motion. In pulling,
the scraper blade is held firmly,
again leaning about 75° to the work surface,
and about 45° to the direction of travel.
In this position, a fast and forceful pull
is given, but hold it right there.
It is not enough just to keep scraping,
you have to feel in your hands if there are
any "hills" and "valleys" and cut the hills
down while flying over the valleys.
Of course, this is an exaggerated
figure of speech, but in essence it is
the function of the hand scraper.
Let us remember the old time cabinetmakers
who veneered with handsawn ebony —
a wood almost impossible to plane — and yet
they could make it as smooth as a mirror.
That is how a scraper can be mastered.
For that kind of rough work, there is today
a *cabinet scraper,* a scraper blade fastened
into a plane-like frame, very good for heavy
work. However, its blade edge is sharpened
to a bevel, like a regular plane blade, and
the burr is drawn after sharpening.
If the scraper produces dust instead
of shavings, it may be that it is not being
held properly, not at the right angles,
and not firmly enough, but chances
are that it is not sharp. It is possible to burnish
the scraper several times without the need
to grind it on the oilstone. First, the burr is
eliminated by holding the burnisher
tight to the surface of the scraper and
pushing it back and forth fast about six or
eight times, or until the burr disappears,
whereupon the burnisher may be
pulled on the edge to draw a new burr,
just as was done the first time.

length of the stone, and pushing back and
forth, holding it vertically and not tilting
the slightest, so that it becomes a perfectly
straight and square (90°) edge. When there
is a slight burr raised, the scraper is laid
flat on the stone and whetted until it is
removed from all four corners. The same is
then repeated on the smooth side of the stone.
The scraper is now laid on the workbench with
the edge sticking over about one inch; while
the left hand is holding it down, the right
hand has to pull the burnisher. (A very good
one can be made by grinding the teeth off an
old sawfile, and making its corners round,
but very important! — it has to be honed as
smooth and shiny as a mirror.) The first
burnishing is to be done lightly at a 90°
angle, the second time a little harder and
the burnisher's angle to the top surface
of the blade should be about 85°,
and the third time still a little harder.
This has to be done to all four corners.
If everything was properly done, there
should be a fine burr on all four corners.

THE BRACE AND BORING

Boring holes in wood is one of the simpler operations in woodworking. There are only a few helpful rules to be observed. When boring with a brace and an auger bit, the bit has to be sharp and in good condition. The left hand holding the head of the brace must be motionless and supply only the power. The right hand does the boring with a cranking motion. The feed screw (the little pointed screw at the end of the auger bit) and the center of the head of the brace have to be parallel with the direction of the hole to be bored, in most cases, at right-angles to the wood. Sighting by eye, or checking with a square should be done quite frequently. In case the wood has to be bored through, only bore until the feed screw comes through on the other side, turn the wood around and bore the rest from that side. If this is not possible, clamp a piece of scrap wood to the backside of the wood. These two methods will prevent splitting of the wood when the bit emerges on the opposite side. Boring and drilling mean the same thing. For making holes in metal, the term drilling is used more frequently, although boring small holes in wood with a hand drill is also called drilling. The two words are interchangeable. Among other purposes, boring may be a shortcut to mortising, doweling, pre-drilling for screws, for jigsaw work, making designs, and the like.

THE SCREWDRIVER

The screwdriver needs no introduction nor any explanations. What it does need is a little more attention. The one that is used to open paint cans, or as a cold chisel to make a hole in brick walls, should not be used for screws. One should have three or four screwdrivers the same sizes as the screws used, in impeccable condition, clean, and sharp. The blade should never be wider than the head of the screw, nor thinner than the slot. These principles are essential to good work.

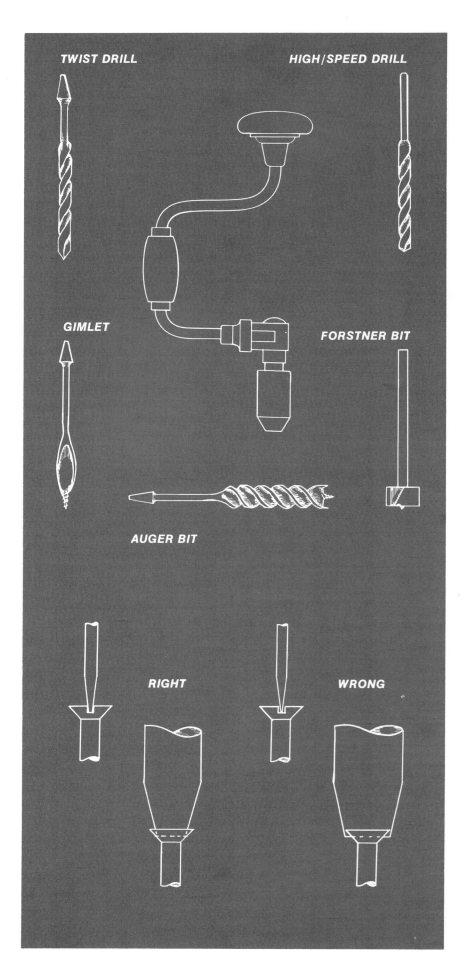

TWIST DRILL

HIGH/SPEED DRILL

GIMLET

FORSTNER BIT

AUGER BIT

RIGHT

WRONG

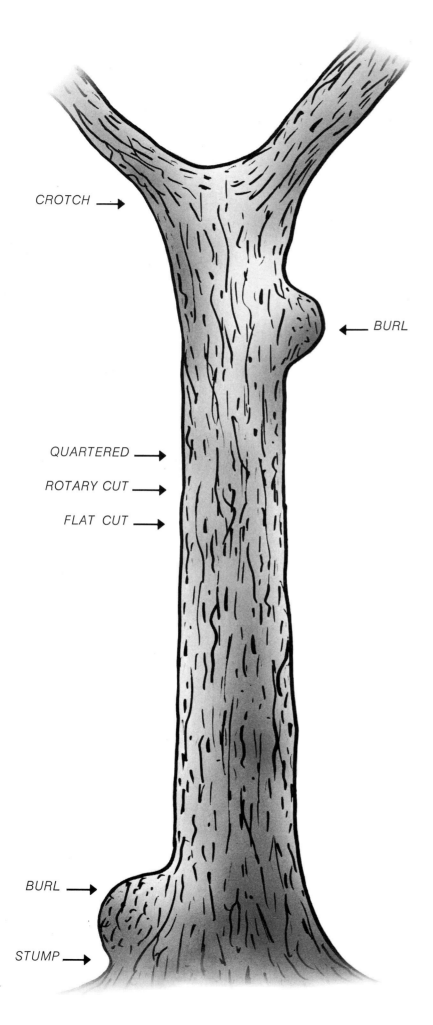

CROTCH →

← BURL

QUARTERED →

ROTARY CUT →

FLAT CUT →

BURL →

STUMP →

WOOD

One of the most wonderful materials nature has provided us with is the wood that we get from trees. These giants of the plant world supply us with many of our vital needs. From oxygen to fruits and nuts, sugar from the maple, turpentine from the terebinth and pine, latex from the rubber tree, even perfumes and medicines are derived from trees. The greatest among the trees of the world are the redwoods of California, the Sequoia. The oldest and largest of them is probably the General Sherman, named by its discoverer in honor of the general. Scientists estimate its age at between 3,000 and 4,000 years. It is about 272 feet high, the height of a modern 25 story building, and the base at ground level is 36 feet in diameter. This tree is the largest and oldest living thing in the world. Wood has been widely used by mankind because, besides being pleasing to the eye, it is a good insulator (low conductor of heat and cold), easy to work, and very durable. Wood never decays, neither from wetness, dryness nor age. Other than fire, Only two things can, and do, destroy wood: fungi which are plants, and insects, such as termites, wood-worms, and wood beetles. Wood has been popularly classified in two groups: hard and soft woods. The broadleaved trees (deciduous) that shed their leaves every year are the hardwoods. The conifers, or evergreens, are the softwoods. This, of course, is not true in all cases, because wouldn't it mean, for example, that fir is a hard softwood and basswood a soft hardwood? Under a microscope, wood is very much like a honeycomb. In hardwood, there are larger water conducting tubes that we call pores, when they are visible. In softwood, however, there are comparatively very narrow, hollow, spindle-shaped fibers. Therefore, we name softwoods nonporous, because the pores can not be seen with the naked eye. As trees grow in height, they also grow in thickness. Each year a new layer is added beneath the bark. The spring growth is thicker and softer than the summer ring, which is harder and narrower.

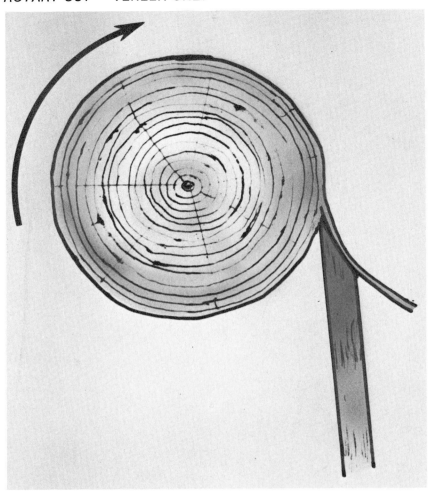

This difference makes it possible for us to tell its age by counting these annual rings on the cross section of a tree. In many trees, the spring growth is of a much lighter, or even a different, color than the summer growth. That is why we have the distinctive graining when a tree trunk is cut into boards or veneer, as in walnut, mahogany, rosewood, zebra wood, teakwood, and many others. Lumber, to be useful for construction of furniture, has to be dried. The old method of air drying is still the best way, but it takes too long, up to two years. Kiln drying takes only hours. Wood, however, is never completely dry. Lumber, especially for making furniture, should have about 6% to 8% moisture content to equal the average vapor pressure of the atmosphere surrounding it. Wood keeps adjusting itself to its environment, to hot, cold, humid, or dry air.

That is why a little (most often temporary) warpage is not a sign of a lack of craftsmanship.

All species of woods have their own characteristic aroma, color, hardness, and weight. An interesting fact is that two of the heaviest woods that sink in water, even when properly seasoned (dried), are ebony, which is almost black, and boxwood, almost white.

Some of the popular softwoods are:

Basswood: a straight-grained, light weight wood with fine texture, very often used for frames, carving, turning, and mouldings.

Cedar: a nicely grained wood which takes a fine finish. Because it is highly resistant to insects (it even repels them), it is used frequently as closet or chest mothproof liners. In this case, it is left unfinished, so that the aroma can emanate from it. Should the aroma weaken in time, a little sandpapering will restore it.

Cypress: a light weight wood, easy to work and practically indestructible by the weather. The most suitable wood for watertanks, hothouses, or any situation where the wood will be subject to extreme heat, cold, or moisture.

Fir: used mostly as structural framing lumber in residential construction, as veneer-core for better grade plywood, and as surface veneer.

Gum: strong, heavy, and often cross-grained, it twists and warps when exposed to moisture or high humidity. It is used chiefly in interiors of commercially mass-produced furniture.

Pine: a very soft wood, easy to work and durable, for interiors and furniture only. It was used extensively in colonial days, and knotty pine is still used in colonial style furniture. It takes a good finish but soaks in a lot of finishing materials. There are many varieties of pine, the best known being Idaho white pine, ponderosa, sugar, and yellow pine.

Redwood: a softwood, it is nonetheless practically indestructible by weather. It resists fungi and insects, and is excellent for exterior use. For interiors, it takes a good finish and is used mainly as beams and panelling.

White Spruce: a light, stiff, and strong wood, it is used in better construction and trim,

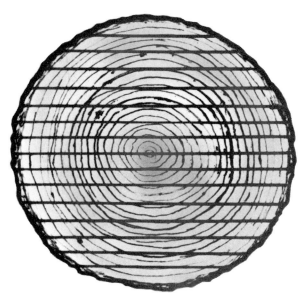

FLAT CUT — LUMBER AND VENEER

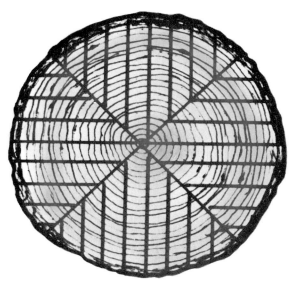

QUARTERED — LUMBER AND VENEER

Some of the popular hardwoods are:

Birch: a hard, heavy, and a tough wood, used for furniture, moldings, and so on. Very often it is stained to imitate the more expensive woods, such as walnut and mahogany. It is the best wood to use for painted furniture.

Cherry: a very hard wood, also used in colonial style furniture. It is very stable after proper seasoning and stains and finishes beautifully.

Elm: a hard wood, very durable, its main feature is that it bends well, which makes it the favorite wood of cabinetmakers, who use it to make many curved parts. *Elm Burl,* because of its overall design of small knots and wavy grain, is a popular veneer for center panels in furniture.

Limba: also known as korina, a beautiful golden yellow wood. It resembles and handles like mahogany in all respects except color.

Mahogany: the preferred wood of cabinetmakers and their customers since the beginning of the 18th century and considered one of the finest woods for furniture. Hard and durable, but comparatively easy to work, it finishes beautifully and has its own luster. It is an excellent wood for carving. Quarter-sawed mahogany has mottled figure, similar to satinwood, and reflects light cast upon it from various angles quite differently.

Maple: a very hard, dense, and fine textured wood. When properly seasoned, it is not subject to warping or shrinking. Maple is the best choice where staining and distressing are required. It also finishes very nicely. *Birdseye Maple,* so called because the whole surface is dotted with very small knot-like spots and a swirling grain. Scientists have no answer for this phenomenon. It is also favored as veneer for center panels and where light furniture is desired.

Teak: a hard, oily, and heavy wood, greatly valued for its beauty and durability. Because of its high oil content, it does not lend itself to glossy finishes. Teak's natural qualities are developed by rubbing with oil or wax.

Walnut: a hard wood, but easily workable, very stable, and quite heavy. Today, walnut is the champion of them all, and for good reasons. It has a distinct grain figure, rich color, and a fine luster under any type of finish.

SOLID versus VENEERED

One of the great misconceptions advanced by furniture hucksters is the term, solid: solid pine, solid maple, solid oak, and so on. There are very few instances where solid lumber is an advantage. Exceptions are chairs, tables, but not the table-tops, furniture frames, and moldings or carvings, which should be solid wood. Also, there may be some cases where, in handcrafted furniture, the design requires solid wood, but that is the extent of it. Even the most stable lumber, if it is in greater width, is apt to have some movement due to changes in its environment. On a well finished surface even the slightest warpage can be very obvious. When solid lumber is glued side by side, to make up a width, it can not be matched for grain or color as veneer can.

THIS IS ALWAYS THE FACE OF A BOARD

LAMINATING

The idea of glueing thin veneers one on top of another at right angles, is a very old one. The Egyptians realized almost five thousand years ago that with this method they could build up and make a larger, more rigid, and stable board. There is a sarcophagus from the Step Pyramid at Saqqara, dating from about 2700 B.C., made up of six layers of about quarter-inch thick veneer, fastened with wooden pegs (the glue must have disappeared). The only problem with the six layers is that the grain of the two surfaces does not run in the same direction. Today's plywood is always made up of an odd number of sheets of veneer. They start out with a center core, then on either side of it go two sheets of veneer across the grain. On top of those, veneer again, in the opposite direction. Always the same way on both sides, so that the stress is equalized and the result is a stable plywood. On the surface, if it is plywood for fine furniture or paneling, veneer is applied, that usually is flitchmatched or bookmatched, where the grain in the veneer coming from the same log match one another. The design is repeated for a beautiful and otherwise unobtainable effect.

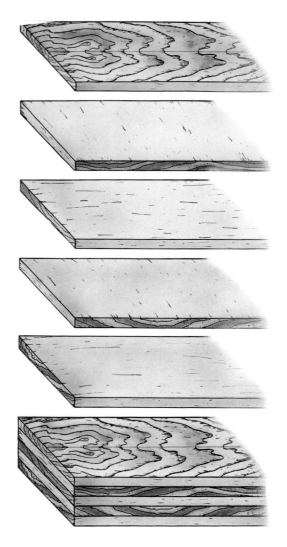

VENEERING

In studying the masterpieces of craftsmen of the past, we have seen an infinite variety of veneerwork designs which may be copied or adapted, or, where it suits the individual project and taste, a new design may be improvised. The big word, of course, is creativity.

Here is a fairly simple design to help you familiarize yourself with the methods and steps involved in veneering. The component parts are cut with a veneer saw, or, if the design calls for curved pieces, with a fine jigsaw. The inlaywork is then assembled and held in place with pins around the edges, leaving enough room to tape the joints. When the pins are removed, the veneer may be handled as a single piece. Apply an even, not too heavy coat of glue to the wood. Position the veneer exactly in place, and tie it down with tape or headless pins so it does not slide.

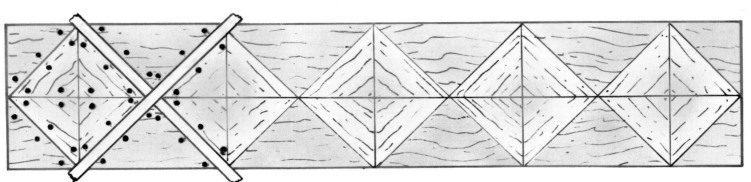

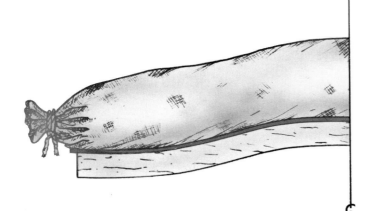

Apply pressure to the veneer and let it dry. If hot glue is used, the sackful of sand should be warm; with cold glue use cold sand. Clamping of course is always preferable, and is easy enough if the piece being veneered is straight. But to make a caul, a snug-fitting curved form for clamping, is a difficult enough job even for a well equipped woodworking shop. An easy method, when using hot glue, is to rub down the veneer with a gluing hammer, which is nothing more than a wood block beveled to a rounded edge with or without a handle. The glue applied to the veneer has to be very thick. Then a drop of glue or water added to the face of the veneer will allow the hammer to slide. In this case the veneer does not have to be taped but can be rubbed down piece by piece. The idea here is to apply a heavy coat of glue to each piece of veneer before setting it in its place, and then to rub it down, squeezing out as much glue as possible until the veneer lays flat. That's all there is to it.
I trust that by now you are able to use the scraper because this is where it is most useful: for scraping the veneerwork of tape, glue and all roughness before it can be sanded with fine sandpaper and polished.

WOOD JOINTS

Joinery is the second big test for the craftsman, the first being the proper and safe use of tools and their upkeep. A well-made joint separates the layman from the craftsman, and the junk from fine furniture. But take heart, it is easier mastered than may appear at first glance.

The BUTT JOINT is the simplest type of joint to make. The only requirement is that all ends are perfectly square. Nails or screws may be used, but it should be kept in mind that nails or screws do not hold very well in the end grain of wood. That is the reason for the metal straps found on primitive chests. However, butt joints are proper, especially today, only for the novice and in rough construction work. They are never used in finer furniture.

The DOWELLED JOINT. Dowels evolved from the pegs that were universally used on primitive furniture and were also popular in Colonial style furniture and construction. Pegs are made by splitting short pieces of straight grained wood with a chisel. They are left square and one end is cut to a point so the peg can be driven into a pre-drilled hole with a hammer. Dowels are rounded pegs the same diameter, or a fraction less, than the drilled hole, to allow space for glue. Because these early carpenters, and their clients, did not trust the glue, even mortise and tenon joints had to be pegged through. Pegs are clearly visible on the surface, a characteristic which, while it enhances certain styles of furniture, does not lend itself to others. Therefore the dowelled joint was developed, where the dowel is hidden from view, yet makes a simple butt into a strong and craftsmanlike joint.

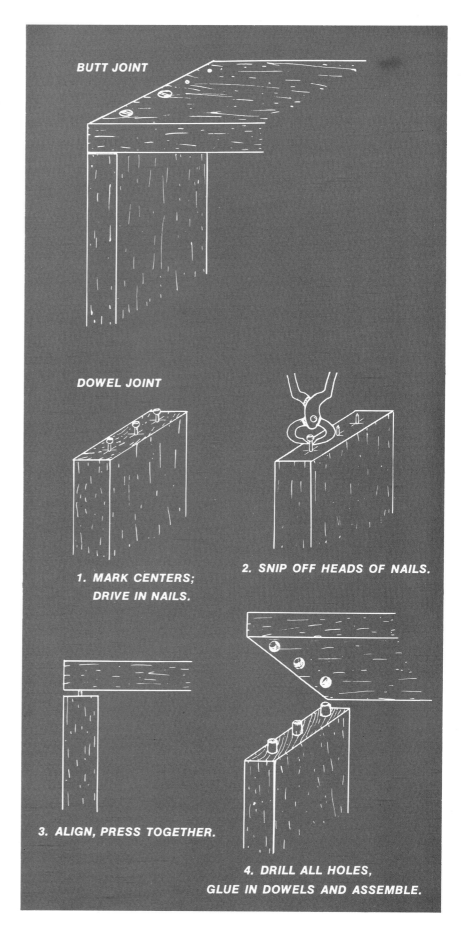

BUTT JOINT

DOWEL JOINT

1. MARK CENTERS; DRIVE IN NAILS.

2. SNIP OFF HEADS OF NAILS.

3. ALIGN, PRESS TOGETHER.

4. DRILL ALL HOLES, GLUE IN DOWELS AND ASSEMBLE.

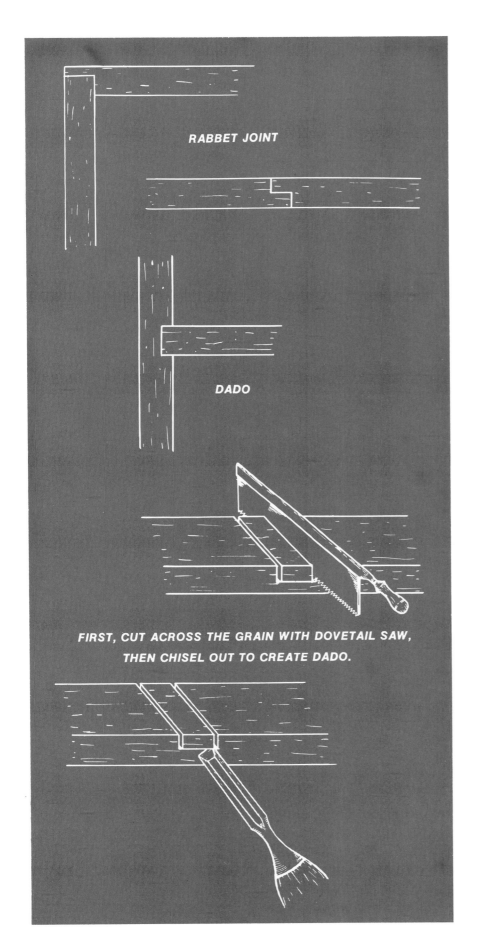

RABBET JOINT

DADO

FIRST, CUT ACROSS THE GRAIN WITH DOVETAIL SAW, THEN CHISEL OUT TO CREATE DADO.

The RABBET JOINT is a great improvement over the butt joint because one of the members is now supported on two sides instead of just one, as in the butt joint. The little additional work is fully justified by the strength gained. However, this still has to be fastened with nails, screws, or preferably, pegs. A rabbet is also used to form a dustproof joint at the edges where cabinet doors meet. In fine construction work all hinged windows and doors should close into a rabbet.

The DADO JOINT. The dado is a groove, usually across the grain of the wood, to receive the full thickness of the piece being joined. It is a useful joint for stationary dividers in cabinets and shelves. Dadoes may be glued without any other fasteners, such as nails, screws, and so on, but if possible they should be clamped while the glue dries. Dadoes are also practically a must in constructing stairs, steps and ladders.

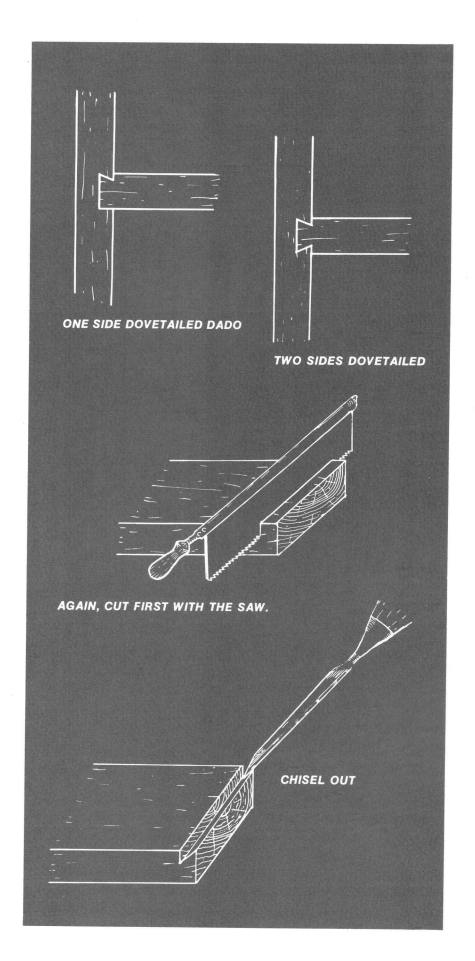

ONE SIDE DOVETAILED DADO

TWO SIDES DOVETAILED

AGAIN, CUT FIRST WITH THE SAW.

CHISEL OUT

The DOVETAILED DADO is one of the finest joints one can make. In this dado one or both sides of the groove are cut at an angle and the piece it receives is cut at a corresponding angle. This joint needs no fasteners, except glue, and it does not even need clamping because it is self-tightening when glued. It makes a superb joint anywhere, even for drawers if the front extends over the sides (but second choice to dovetailing) because it cannot be used at corners.

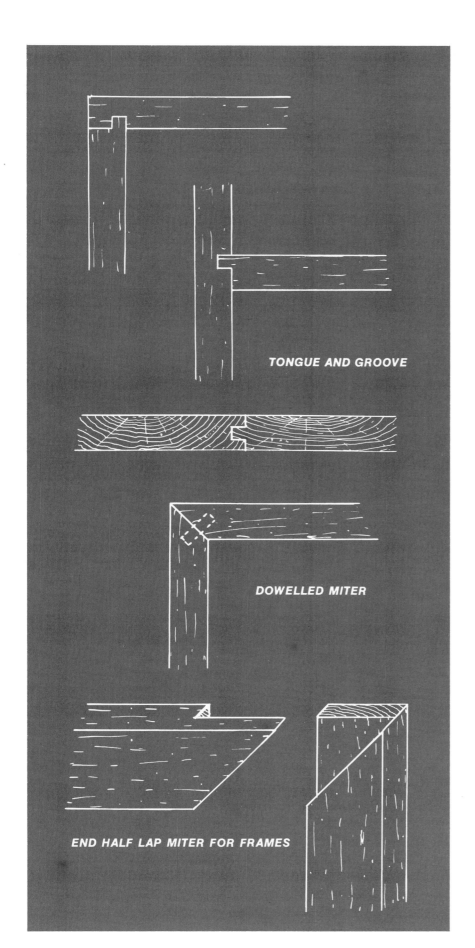

TONGUE AND GROOVE

DOWELLED MITER

END HALF LAP MITER FOR FRAMES

The TONGUE AND GROOVE is similar to a
straight dado, with the difference being
that here the groove is narrower and
the piece it receives has a shoulder,
or, if it is an edge joint,
two shoulders, which makes for
a firmer and more precise joint.

The MITER. Each member is cut to an exact
45° angle and when put together they create a
perfect 90° corner, which we call a square
corner. A miter, like a butt joint, needs to
be fastened, either with dowels or splines

MORTISE AND TENON

1. MARK LENGTH OF TENONS WITH SQUARE AND PENCIL.

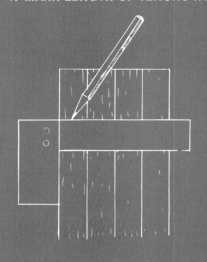

2. MARK THICKNESS OF TENON WITH GAUGE.

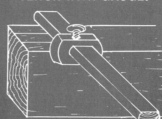

3. CUT TENON ON THE OUTSIDE OF GAUGE LINE.

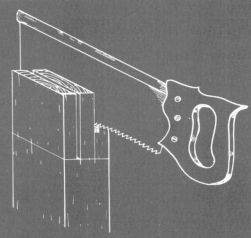

4. CUT SHOULDERS, LEAVING PENCIL MARK ON THE FACE BUT CUTTING INTO IT AT THE TENON.

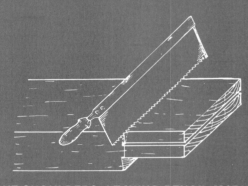

5. CUT MORTISE ON THE INSIDE OF THE GAUGE LINE.

6. CHISEL OUT MORTISE FROM BOTH SIDES.

7. OPEN MORTISE AND TENON ASSEMBLED.

8. HAUNCHED-HIDDEN MORTISE AND TENON GIVES ADDITIONAL STRENGTH TO TABLES.

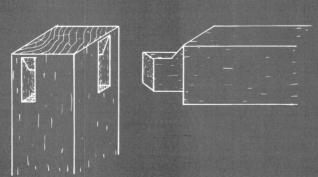

9. SECTION AT JUNCTION OF ASSEMBLED TABLE LEG AND APRONS.

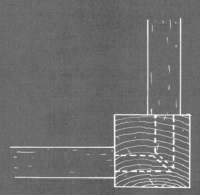

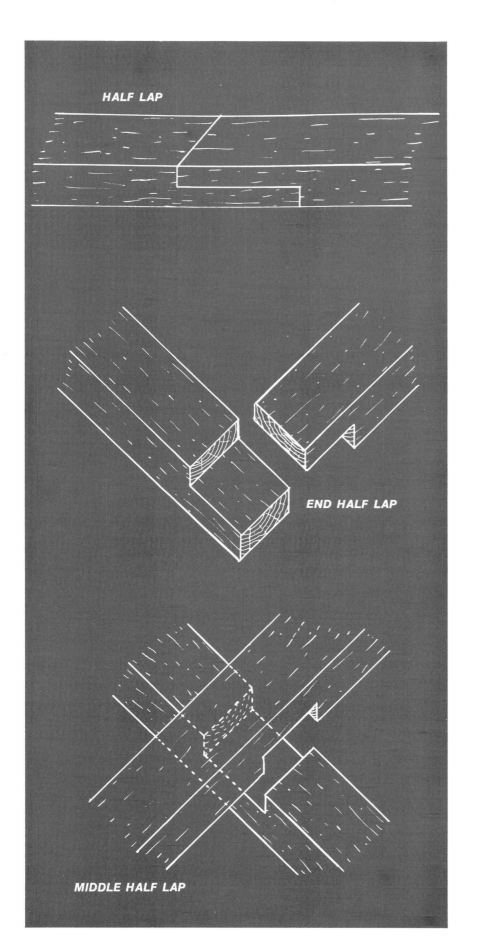

HALF LAP

END HALF LAP

MIDDLE HALF LAP

The MORTISE AND TENON is the grand-daddy of all joints. Actually most joints derive from or are variations of the mortise and tenon, which is obviously the best joint for all kinds of frames, including chairs, tables, doors, windows, and many more. A warning note: if you would like a tight joint, try not to cut away the pencil or gauge mark.

The HALF LAP is a simplified version of the mortise and tenon. In this, however, both members are cut to exactly half the thickness of the wood. When glued and clamped well it is a good joint, but relies completely on glue.

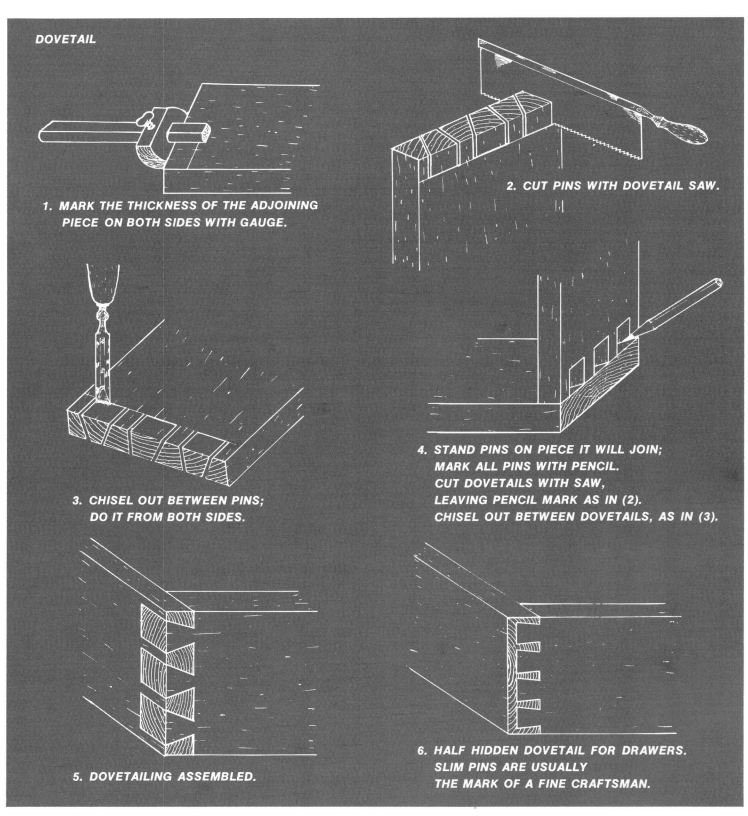

DOVETAIL

1. MARK THE THICKNESS OF THE ADJOINING PIECE ON BOTH SIDES WITH GAUGE.

2. CUT PINS WITH DOVETAIL SAW.

3. CHISEL OUT BETWEEN PINS; DO IT FROM BOTH SIDES.

4. STAND PINS ON PIECE IT WILL JOIN; MARK ALL PINS WITH PENCIL. CUT DOVETAILS WITH SAW, LEAVING PENCIL MARK AS IN (2). CHISEL OUT BETWEEN DOVETAILS, AS IN (3).

5. DOVETAILING ASSEMBLED.

6. HALF HIDDEN DOVETAIL FOR DRAWERS. SLIM PINS ARE USUALLY THE MARK OF A FINE CRAFTSMAN.

The DOVETAIL. A hand made dovetail joint is the high mark of craftsmanship. Its good appearance and extreme strength make it a most desirable joint, especially in drawer construction. It is also very useful for all kinds of boxes, cabinets, and chests. Dovetailing has always been the pride of master craftsmen because making it properly requires skill and patience. A commode was acknowledged to be of fine workmanship if its drawers were well dovetailed. However, the technique can be mastered easily enough with a little practice.

GLUES AND GLUEING

Until very recently, the glue used for thousands of years, and in many parts of the world still used, has been animal glue, popularly known as hot glue. This glue is a gelatinous matter obtained from the hides, bones, and other parts of cattle and oxen that contain gelatin. These are soaked in limewater to remove the hair and fatty materials, then removed from the limewater and boiled down to a jelly, strained, cleaned, and allowed to dry out into thin sheets. Before the craftsman can use it, he has to melt it down and cook it. The best way is to let it soak for at least six hours, or better overnight, and then bring it to the boiling point in a double boiler (the outer pot filled with boiling water, the inner containing the glue). It then becomes a viscous substance ready to be used.

For hardwoods, the glue should be thin, about the consistency of milk, for example. For softwoods, it may be a little heavier. For veneering in clamps, it should be like heavy cream, and for use when veneering by hand about as heavy as buttermilk. When using hot glue, it is always advisable to warm the wood first, just slightly, but not too hot, so that the glue does not freeze before it has a chance to penetrate the wood fibers. Clamping is also very important for this reason. There should not be a thick layer of glue in the joint, the two pieces of wood have to touch each other with the thinnest imaginable film of glue in between that reaches into the fibers of each piece and holds them together like millions of little hooks.

A well glued joint will last forever. Animal glue and wood are very compatible because they are similar natural substances. Wood is also a gel in a solidified form. Of the many modern glues and cements available, most are very good in woodworking. Their use is usually explained on the container. Some are very fast working, but that is what our hurry-up civilization demands, isn't it?

FINISHING

To preserve and enhance the natural beauty of wood, and also to protect it from daily use and abuse, many different kinds of finishes were developed, from oil finish to (because of our strange fascination for glittering things) high gloss lacquer finish. The oldest and still the best is the oil finish. It is done with boiled linseed oil (that is how it is bought, never attempt to boil it), since raw linseed oil dries very slowly and goes through a gummy-sticky stage before drying. After the piece is sandpapered smooth, give it a heavy coat of oil. Let it soak in for about fifteen or twenty minutes, then wipe it completely dry. Twenty-four or preferably forty-eight hours later sandpaper it with a very fine finishing paper, at least No. 220 or finer, and oil again. This should be done a minimum of three times. For a beautiful low gloss, water resistant, even somewhat alcohol proof finish, this procedure should be followed once a month for at least six months. Then sandpapering may be replaced by a good rubdown with 000 steel wool, before each oiling. This may sound funny, but oil finish is self-healing. If a minor scratch or dent occurs, the oil from below the surface will come up, because of the changes in pressure, I suppose, and fill up the bruised fibers and the damage all but disappears. A very important safety precaution: all rags used in oil finishing MUST be soaked in water and hung up to air-dry before disposal. Beware of spontaneous combustion!

WOOD STAINS AND STAINING

For all practical purposes, there are three kinds of wood stains: oil, alcohol, and water stain. Their purpose is to change the color of wood, or darken it to a desired effect, without hiding the grain of the wood. Oil stain consists of oil pigments, such as raw and burnt umber, raw and burnt sienna, lampblack, and so on. They are ground in oil and thinned with linseed oil and turpentine. Oil stain is applied heavily, allowed to soak in for a few minutes, then wiped dry. If any oil base finish goes over it, such as linseed oil or varnish, the wood gets a shellac sealer first. Alcohol stain is made by dissolving aniline colors in alcohol. This stain is used primarily in refinishing, where there may be old filler or finish left in the pores. This will color it, but it takes experience to apply alcohol stain, because it dries almost instantly and overlapping may show up as darker spots. If an alcohol base finish, such as shellac or French polish is intended, an oil base sealer, linseed oil or varnish, must be applied first. Water stain is best left to the manufacturers of cheap furniture. It is inexpensive, fairly easy to apply, but it raises the grain of the wood. After drying, it must be sanded again, which may remove some of the stain, which then requires another coating, and so on and on.

VARNISH FINISH

Originally varnish was derived from fossil gum, and other gums derived from trees, mixed with linseed oil, but today this has been replaced almost completely by synthetic resins. Varnish is an extremely durable finish. Where furniture or woodwork is exposed to a lot of use and weather a varnish finish is definitely advisable. The application of varnish, while it is an easy procedure, does require a few very important precautions. It must be done in a clean room, as dust free as possible; a very clean, preferably new, brush, and a new can of varnish should be used. The wood should be well sanded, and sealed with a coat of thinned shellac (one-third denatured alcohol to two-thirds of four

pound cut shellac); after drying, this sealcoat is sanded with a very fine sandpaper and wiped clean. For easier working, the varnish may be thinned with one-fourth pure turpentine. If at all possible the piece to be varnished should lay horizontal. Brush on varnish from end to end as the grain of the wood runs, starting from the far edge away from you. When the whole surface is covered with an even coat start at one end and with the tip of the brush only, brush across the grain from edge to edge and end to end lightly and quickly. Following that, brush it out again lengthwise from end to end. This will eliminate bubbles and even out the finish. It is a good idea to do this work in the evening or just before quitting time, so that no dust is raised to settle on the fresh varnish. When doing a whole cabinet apply varnish sparingly, so that it does not run down the vertical surfaces. Allow at least forty-eight hours for thorough drying; then rub down with No. 400 sandpaper lubricated with plenty of water, and wipe dry. If a heavier finish is desired you can give the piece another coat, or even two, in this manner. (If there is enough varnish left in the can to be worth saving, close the lid very tightly and store it upside down.) After the last sandpaper rubdown, wax lightly with a good paste wax and enjoy!

SHELLAC

Shellac, a resin, is produced by an insect that lives in trees in the Far East. It is not a very durable finish by itself, except maybe for cabinet interiors, or where it is not exposed to much use or wear. (It is better when applied as French polish.) Brushed on in one or two even coats, followed after drying with a rubbing with 000 steel wool dipped in paste wax and polished with a soft cloth, it will give a passable finish.

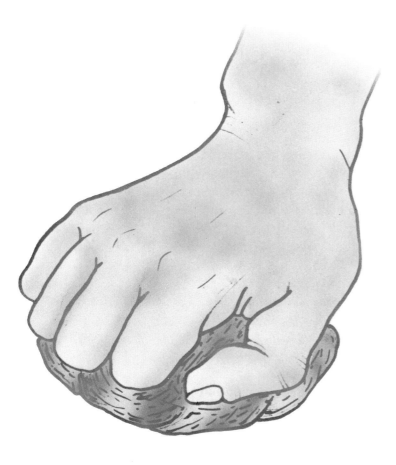

FRENCH POLISHING

French polishing, as it was done during and since the 18th century, is a tricky business. If you have followed this book this far, however, I am sure you can master it in a short time. Apprentices in the olden days would start by doing the insides of cabinets and the ground-work on the exteriors, such as filling and building up the finish, but the final polishing was only done by the craftsman. The keyword throughout French polishing, to be emphasized again and again, is FEELING: not in the emotional sense (even that would help) but in the hands and in the amount of pressure that should be applied and the speed that must be maintained. Neither too fast nor too slow and the reason for it will be clear later, but let us say very much like a waltz in moderate three-quarter time.

I remember a time when the whole shop was doing French polishing and they were whistling and singing waltzes to keep the rhythm of polishing. The boss would urge them on once-in-a-while with, "Why don't you sing a Csardas (fast Hungarian folk music) instead?" To get back to the work at hand, the process begins like this: All surfaces are wetted down with a damp rag. After they are dry, they are sanded with a very fine sandpaper, the equivalent of 4/0. A ball is made of cotton rags, about the size of a tennis ball or smaller, to fit the hand. (At one time we tried old silk stockings but they let the polish out too fast.) Pour a little polish onto it, one-third alcohol to two-thirds shellac, to start; later it has to be thinner. Hit the ball on a piece of scrap wood until about one-third of it is flat. Again pour about a tablespoonful of polish onto the flattened part of the ball, and cover it with a piece of cotton rag. As this wears, you will have to keep changing this outer rag, but always lift this when adding polish. Gather all corners of the rag in your hand, so that the flattened part of the ball is nice and firm. Now you can start padding the work surface, pressing the ball firmly against the wood, but not too hard. It should feel as if you are putting about two pounds of weight on the ball. Go the whole length of the wood from end to end, each stroke next to the other, adding more polish to the ball as you go along, until there is a sheen on the surface. Let it rest a few minutes. You may now catch your breath and accept congratulations. You have just passed the first test and you are ready for initiation into ASSOFP, The Ancient Secret Society of Furniture Polishers. To continue, have on hand some finely ground pumice stone, or preferably two chunks, and some pure lemon oil. If you have chunks, rub them together above the work surface so as to deposit some fine powder on it, or use the powdered form sparingly. This is necessary to fill the pores. Sprinkle on a few drops of the lemon oil. Add more polish onto the ball, and from now on do not ever stop the ball on the work surface. If you have to stop, lift it off fast or slide it off. With the same pressure as used previously, but now making rows of circles, about 6-8 inches in diameter, keep adding polish and lemon oil, both sparingly. Work the ball out almost dry. If the pores did not fill, you may add pumice once more. The right amount of oil needed can be established in the following way: if you feel the ball sticking and it is hard to pull, there is not enough oil. There is too much oil if the ball leaves a shiny trace and slides too easily. In this case, just keep on working until it disappears. When the amount of oil is right you will feel it holding on to the finish lightly and a shadow will be following your ball. For variety, you can make the figure eight instead of circles. If you have stopped the motion of the ball in one spot, have too much polish on the ball, or for any other reason burned the accumulated finish (there is a muddy spot) do not despair. Let it dry about fifteen minutes. Rub with No. 0000 steel wool and a few drops of lemon oil until it is smooth again. Continue polishing. When the pores are filled and there is a fair amount of finish on the surface, it is best to let it stand for a day. Continue the same way, except now you can thin the polish to half alcohol and half shellac. You should also very gradually ease up on the pressure, until you decide you have a heavy enough finish on the surface. Keep thinning the polish and do not add more oil. Finally, pour a few drops of alcohol onto the ball, put a clean rag on it and do it again with straight strokes from end to end, until all shadow disappears. Now, stand back, accept the applause of your admirers, hang a big medallion on your neck, and have both your cheeks kissed. You do deserve the accolade because you are a craftsman and a creator of things that give pleasure and enjoyment to others.

There is no greater gift one can give to loved ones and friends than the giving of himself . . . the fruit of his mind and skillful hands.

Laszlo Katz is from the land of creaky old castles, Transylvania, where in the late 1930's skilled trades and craftsmanship were still respected endeavors. One of the few of the last generation of cabinetmakers, he began his three-year apprenticeship at the age of fourteen, with the good fortune to be under the tutelage of a master craftsman who had worked for a time in Paris. This artisan instilled in his student the admiration for the great cabinetmakers who were the glory of France in the olden days, a reverence which stayed with him since his youth, prompting a deep interest in the history of furniture and cabinetmaking. Today, operating his own woodworking shop, he includes among his clients some of the finest designers, architects, and decorators, as well as fellow cabinetmakers who turn to him with their problem jobs, or simply for advice. To Laszlo Katz cabinetmaking is not merely a trade that provides his livelihood, but truly a labor of love.